"THE MADNESS"

Memoir of a Piano Tuner

TERENCE LOWE

FORWARD

Serendipity, fate, call it what you like, a force which cannot be explained governs all our lives. In this little book I tell the tale of mine. By chance, at the age of just fifteen I started my apprenticeship learning how to tune and maintain the master of all musical instruments, the piano!

By the time I was twenty, I was working for the piano-maker Steinway and Sons in London, tuning pianos for the BBC, all the capitol's concert halls and recording studios. Tuning and preparing pianos for artists such as André Previn, Daniel Barenboim, Alfred Brendal, Vladimir Ashkenazi and Pink Floyd. I then became the sole piano tuner-technician for the Viennese piano-maker Bosendorfer, preparing pianos for John Ogden, Pete Townshend and Oscar Peterson.

By the mid nineteen seventies I was working for myself, taking off the collar and tie, letting my hair grow and becoming the piano tuner for most of the eminent recording studios in and around London. Tuning pianos for the impresario Harvey Goldsmith, for artists such as David Bowie, Queen, Crosby, Stills, Nash and Young, Bob Dylan, the list goes on… and on.

Towards the end of the nineteen seventies I had returned from the Caribbean island of Montserrat, where I had been looking after the studio piano for George Martin. There were a few outings with The Who, including visiting the Cannes Film Festival. Then I was in the ill-fated last tour of the band Wings. Paul

McCartney got locked up in jail for smuggling drugs into Japan. I was in Charing Cross Hospital with a life-threatening disease. I survived. After my recovery I left London and the razzmatazz, to live a quiet life in the country.

In the early nineties I was commissioned to restored Keith Richards Psychedelic grand piano in my Totnes workshop. Soon after this I lost my home and business, taking up a semi-feral existence, eventually living on an old boat on the banks of the beautiful river Dart in Devon. The boat was given in lieu of money owed for work done on a piano.

I have now worked on pianos, making my living for fifty years. I have been very lucky learning such a skill, taking me to so many places, meeting so many interesting people and best of all, being independent throughout any fateful events.

Terry the Tuner

THE FIRST STEP
TO HARMONY

My first introduction to playing a musical instrument was learning to play the Cornet, with the local brass band. I was loaned an instrument, a very old silver plated Cornet which I was taught how to blow so as to get a note and one of the first lessons was how to maintain and look after the instrument. I had to polish the Cornet with silver polish, then to wash out the inside of the instrument with soapy water and finally oil all the valves and slides. I enjoyed this weekly maintenance just as much as learning to play. After a couple of years, I was starting to sit in and play second Cornet with the Band, when my parents, yet again, decided to move house. I sadly had to return my Cornet to the Brass band for someone else to learn.

I now turned my attention to my newly acquired guitar, having received it for a Christmas present. The steel strung acoustic had a white front and I so wanted a red one. I was packing things into boxes, contents of the garden shed, ready for moving to a new house when I found a small tin of red paint. On the label it read Japanese lacquer. I opened the tin lid, it was just the colour I wanted my guitar. I removed the strings and all the fittings. I opened the tin and with a loaded paintbrush started to apply the lacquer to the front of my guitar. As I applied the last brushstrokes, a fly landed on my wet finish. I used my finger to remove the offending insect. As I did this, I smudged the finish. I tried to brush out the offending marks from the quickly drying lacquer. This made things worse. As I looked at the mess I was in, I realised that there was a slight colour change giving the finish a depth to look into. Now using only my fingertips, swirling them around, I was well proud of my new effect finish on my new guitar.

As I was cleaning my hands, having propped my guitar against my bedroom wall leaving it to dry, my Father was shouting for me to get packing the contents of the shed. As I did not respond quick enough, he burst through my bedroom door, greeting me with the proverbial backhander. He then saw my guitar and said, "What have you done?" In a flash he picked it up by the neck and smashed it over my head, this was followed by several more blows until he was just holding the neck of the instrument.

After moving it was yet again time to start a new school. The schools I attended in the West Riding of Yorkshire were all very tough. My new school was the toughest. On my first day I received a bloody nose, a punch in the stomach and much taunting for being the new boy. I had learnt to hold my own against the bullies after my Grandmother told me "Not to forget I had the Attersley arm". I asked her "What was the Attersley arm?" She told me that when she was young, her uncle was a bare fisted fighter with quite a reputation, and that if you took a punch from him, you didn't get up.

Later in my first week in the new school, there was a period of games, the changing rooms being a very vulnerable time for anyone getting knocked about. I had just removed my blazer when I was pulled around by one of the school bullies. As I turned my Grandmothers words echoed through my head. In a fraction of a second, I pulled back my fist and delivered a punch straight up at my taller opponent's nose. It was like going into slow motion. His nose exploded in blood followed by instant tears. I was left alone, for a while, after this incident but I did receive six of the best from the Headmaster. One could fight back against bullies but not against the teachers, who would regularly pull someone out of the class for six of the best. The whistling cane striking the flesh of the upturned palm of the hand. I was regularly pulled out of the class by the music master, a Mr Fullylove, for a good slap over the backside with the slipper. As a part of every music lesson we had to gather around the grand piano and while being conducted and accompanied, we would sing songs. While singing away my eyes gazed over the inside of the classroom grand piano, watching the hammers bobbing up and down. I could see where the string wrapped around a pin. I realised the pins were for tuning. After the singing, while everyone was returning to their seats, I stuck my head inside the grand piano looking at the tuning pins. I realised that I had a ring spanner that would fit them.

The next music lesson was the first class after lunch-break. I entered the music room early. In my pocket were three different ring spanners. I quickly found one that fitted the tuning pins. I managed to turn several of them which were all very tight. I put the spanners back in my pocket and sat down at my desk. The lesson started with the usual gathering around the grand piano. As Mr Fullylove played the first chords of the song, the whole class started laughing at the obvious out of tune notes. The teacher went into a rage. He started pulling, by the ear, one boy at random saying "Was it you, Boy?!" As he pulled my ear the spanners in my pocket clanged together. I was ordered to empty my pockets. In a flash he realised I was the offender. This time I was delivered the most vicious six of the best I had ever had.

At the beginning of July 1966, I made the first big conscious decision of my life. On my way home from school, walking alone, the thought came into my head, "I'm never going back there", even though my birthday was some weeks ahead. I was still only fourteen but was adamant about my decision. When I arrived home, I told my mother I was never going back to school. At that point my father came home from work. I told him of my decision. Immediately he went into one of his rants, shouting, "You bloody fool, you'll be a nothing!" Later after tea, my father was still ranting, and my mother was reading the evening paper. Suddenly she said, with a hint of excitement, "Young man wanted to learn the business of tuning and repairing pianos". This, to me, sounded most interesting, as my mother knew of my love for music, having learned to play the cornet with the Thurlston Silver Prize Brass Band four years earlier. I always wanted a piano, but never could have one as my mum and dad were always moving and the bother of moving a heavy piano was out of the question.

The next day my mother telephoned Messrs Wilson and Peck, the company that placed the advert. She explained that I was not quite fifteen, this, at the time, being the legal age that one could leave school. The reply was, "Bring him along anyway", emphasising that my mother was to come to the interview as well. An appointment for 10 am on the following Monday, a week before my fifteenth birthday. On the day, my mother and myself caught the bus to the centre of Sheffield and alighted right opposite Wilson and Peck's. This was a large building on four floors. We entered through the heavy mahogany and glass doors and were greeted by a well-dressed man in a pin-striped suit with a carnation in his lapel button-hole. The man said to my mother "Could I help you Madam". My mother replied "Yes, we are here for an interview with a Mr Fair". "Ah yes" he said, "That would be my brother". The man escorted my mother and myself to the first floor. As the lift door opened, we were greeted by a sea of grand pianos. My mother and I were led down an avenue of grand pianos on one side and upright pianos on the other and ushered towards a huge carved desk. "This is the young man and his mother" our escort told the man sitting down. The man stood up and shook my mother's hand. We were asked to sit down. After some basic questions about me, what my basic interests were, I told him I liked music and woodwork. Out of the blue he asked, "Does he have fits?" My mother assured him I did not have fits. He then told us of one young man they had employed who regularly had epileptic fits and they did not want anyone else who had such a condition. He then said that he could offer me the post of Trainee Piano Repairer and Tuner. The hours were 8 am until 5 pm and 9 am till 1 pm on Saturdays, and the wage he could offer me was two pounds and ten shillings per week for the first six months. I could start on the first Monday after my fifteenth birthday.

The next couple of weeks I spent my time doing the things I liked most. Fishing, bike rides and playing the guitar. Monday morning came for my first day at work. I caught the bus early and arrived in time to walk through the doors at five minutes to eight. I was greeted by a porter wearing an apron and a flat cap. He said, "Good morning, can I help you?" I told him that I was here to start work. He said, "Follow me" and showed me to a tiny office situated under the huge staircase which led to the first floor. He said, "You had better wait here until Mr Fair arrives". The interior of the room was lined with shiny mahogany and there was a table and two chairs. On the wall there was a noticeboard with the days of the week at the top. At various intervals delivery notes were pinned-up for pianos sold and pianos to be collected. At eight-thirty prompt the Fair brothers arrived. The porter had told them that I had arrived, and I was shown to the lift to where Mr Fair stood. The lift door opened, he stepped in and I followed. We ascended to the top floor, four stories up.

As the lift door opened, I was greeted by smells and noises I had never experienced before. The whole of the top floor was partitioned into four separate workshops, with glass in every partition from the waist upwards so one could see everyone working from one end to the other. I followed Mr Fair to a workshop at the end of the floor. He opened the door, one of the new smells got stronger. There were three benches at which there was a man working at each one. Behind them stood the piano they were working on. Mr Fair said "Good morning Tom, Harry and Albert. This is the new boy". Tom came over and shook my hand and said to Mr Fair "Leave him with us". Mr Fair left and went to inspect the other workshops.

Tom introduced me to Harry and Albert. Tom said, "Have you got an apron?" I said "Yes" and took out my old school wood-working apron. Tom was the workshops foreman and he gave me my first job. He showed me to a door which led to the top of a spiral staircase. On the landing was a small stool and a large block of wood, three of four old boxes with sheets of newspaper, brown paper and tissue paper and various pieces of card. Tom sat on the stool and picked up a hammer and a round piece of metal about six inches long. Tom said, "This is a punch" and proceeded to fold a newspaper and place it on top of the block of wood. He placed the punch on top of the paper and struck it hard twice with the hammer. He then put down the ham-mer and picked up an old bodkin with the point filed off. He pushed it through a small hole on the side of the punch and out came several perfectly formed paper washers with a small hole in the middle. He handed me the hammer and the punch and said, "Can you do that?" I said "Yes" and proceeded with my first blow and then my second. I put the hammer down and pushed the bodkin through the hole and hey presto, paper washers. I asked Tom what they were for. He replied that "This particular size was for using as shims to regulate the depth of touch on the keys of the piano. He then showed me a smaller punch. He said "The smaller washers are for the levelling of the keys on a piano. The different thicknesses, from thin card to brown paper, news-paper and finally stiff tissue for the finest of adjustments. Tom said, "There is a box for each size and each thickness". Then Tom said, "Do as many as you can, I'll be back presently". I proceeded with my chore. After about an hour and a half I stopped to give my arm a rest. I stood up, had a stretch and peered down the staircase. You could see it spiral all the way to the bottom of the building, four floors below.

About an hour later the door opened and Harry walked through. "Come on" he said, "This will be your job from tomorrow". "What's that?" I asked. He replied, "Making the tea". Harry showed me to a small room. In it there were two old gas stoves, each with two large ancient cast iron kettles. "This one's ours'" said Harry. On a table was a tray with four pint sized white mugs. "This is how we have our tea here" he said. He proceeded to put a heaped teaspoon of loose tea into each mug, followed by a teaspoon of thick tinned condensed milk. Our kettle had boiled, and he filled each pint pot. He picked up the tray and went back to our workshop. "Tea up!" said Harry. This was an alien way of making tea, but I did not question the method. Tom, by now, had taken off his apron and put his suit jacket on. It was an old and threadbare pinstriped suit with a white shirt and a red tie. After we had finished our tea break, Tom, with his small brown leather case said he was off to tune the piano at the City Hall for an evening concert. Tom left instructions with Harry for me to help him until he returned. After Tom had left, I asked Harry "What's that smell?" Harry and Albert both laughed. "It's the glue pot" said Harry. He then showed me, on a gas ring, on which stood a cast iron pot, about the size of a bucket with an inner part. I peered in. I could see hot steamy brown glue about the consistency of treacle. "This is animal glue" said Harry and then proceeded to show me an old sweet jar with a screw top. Inside were thousands of tiny shiny brown pellets. He put his hand in the jar and took out a handful and emptied them into the hot glue pot. He then put half a pint of water in and gave it a stir. He said, "That'll be ready in an hour".

Harry had placed a high stool next to his alongside his bench. On Tom's bench lay trays made of wood, each about four feet long and six inches wide. Placed on the trays were all the parts of the piano workings. Harry told me the name of the piano mechanism was called the 'action'. Tom picked up the first hammer of one of the long wooden trays and said, "Watch carefully". He then took a small metal device with a handle. Placed the bottom of the hammer on the bed of the device and pressed a handle. A metal pin came down and pushed a tiny metal pin out of its hole. A small piece of wood then separated, it was U-shaped with a hole for a screw and two tiny holes on each side with a red felt bush. Tom said that they call this a flange. He then placed the flange and the hammer on the wooden tray. Each hammer and flange were both numbered. Next, Harry said "You have a go". I picked up the hammer and placed it on the device known as the de-centering machine. I lined up the pin hole and pushed the lever down with more pressure than I anticipated. The pin popped out. "Good" said Harry, "Now do the rest". I looked along the line of hammers and picked up the last one. The number read 88. I set about my task. At first it was slow. But as I gained the feel of the job my speed picked up. Beside me Tom did the next operation, which was to reamer out the tiny felt bushes in the flange and fit a new pin into the bushes. This was done with a long needle with rough sides known as a broach. This was pushed through the two holes of the flange ready for the new pin to be fitted. Harry tested each one. He knew that if it was too loose it would rattle, and if the bush was too stiff the note would stick.

Above Tom's bench there were shelves full of trays of piano parts in need of similar attention. Eighty-eight of this and eighty-eight of that. I finished de-centering the last hammer just as Tom returned from his tuning at the City Hall. It was now lunchtime. Tom said, "Do you have your snap?", "I have sandwiches" I replied. Tom, Harry and Albert, all at the stroke of 1 pm, clearly heard from the town hall clock, started to eat their lunch. Not a word was said until everyone had finished. Tom and Harry lit cigarettes while Albert stoked-up his pipe. With over half an hour before resuming work I asked if I could go and have a look around. Tom said, "Only on this floor today". I left our workshop and looked in next door. There was a very old man, a much younger man and a boy roughly my age. At the next workshop were big double doors. As I went closer the doors opened. Through it came a man in his apron and his sleeves rolled-up. "Who are you?" he asked. "I'm the new boy in Tom's workshop" I replied. The man held out his hand. We shook hands and he said "My name is Mr White and I'm the head French Polisher. Come in and have a look around". I followed Mr White through the double doors. A workshop full of light greeted me. As the building curved around a corner, this workshop was enormous. There was a total of eight dormer windows, each with a bench in front. There was a total of eight French polishers plus four apprentices. Each man was working on one piano, some on up-right pianos and some on grand pianos. I then heard the town hall clock strike two and immediately everyone started work. I briskly returned to my workshop.

Tom was tying on his apron as I walked through the door. "Right" he said, "You can polish keys this afternoon". On Tom's bench was a set of piano keys. At the end of the bench was a vice with wooden claws covering the jaws. Tom took the first key and placed it in the wooden jaws and tightened the device. He then picked up a block of wood an inch thick, about eight inches long and four inches wide. Glued to one side was a piece of hard thick felt. "Now watch me" said Tom. Holding the felt side up, he took a few fingers full of white powder and spread it evenly over the pad of felt. Then from an old bottle, with a small hole pierced in the screw top, he splashed methylated spirits over the white powder. "Not too wet, not too dry" said Tom. He then turned over the block and started polishing the ivory key from side to side, backwards and forwards and round and round. After several minutes Tom stopped. He then wiped, with the palm of his hand, the key clean. He released the key from the vice and with a white rag, dampened with meths, to clean-up any residue from the wooden key. Picking up the next key in line he put the two together in the light of the window. The key Tom had polished, compared with the other, had transformed a dirty yellow, rough feeling ivory key into one which was pearly white and silky smooth with a mirror gloss finish. It was now my turn. I took the next key in line, placed it in the vice, took the polishing block and started to mimic Tom's actions. It was about fifteen minutes before I got anywhere near the finish Tom had attained. For the rest of the afternoon I polished the ivory tops until my arms ached. I was relieved when five o'clock came. Everyone took off their aprons and put on their coats. Tom, Harry and Albert all wore hats. Tom, a black bowler, Harry a trilby and Bert a brown flat cap. We left the workshop, Tom last; he switched off the lights and locked the door. Everyone waited for the lift. As the lift went down to the ground floor, Tom asked "How did you like your first day?" I replied, "Very much, thank you". We all walked out of the building, everyone said goodnight and we went our separate ways. I walked to the bus stop, caught the bus home. My first day at work.

OCTAVES AND UNISONS

O ver the next few weeks I learned more about the workings of the various types of pianos. Uprights came in three different designs. Overstrung were considered the best. This is where the strings are stretched at an angle across the instrument, bass and treble strings crossing over one another. This gave the maximum length of string in a limited space within the case design, thus giving the best possible tone. Other upright pianos came with the strings all in the same direction. These were known as oblique or straight strung. This is where all the strings simply go from top to bottom. As in all pianos the treble strings are the shortest and also the thinnest, and the bass strings the longest and fattest. Although I was slowly becoming more familiar with upright pianos, I had not yet touched any grand pianos.

Over this period, in my lunch break, I explored more of the musical building. Wilson and Peck Ltd boasted the largest piano and organ show rooms in the provinces. On the ground floor was a taste of everything, pianos, organs, radiograms and televisions. In its own separate area were the woodwind and brass instruments. My favourite department was the guitars and amplifiers. On the first floor was the main piano showroom, on the third floor was the organ room. There were Hammond organs, harmoniums and small pipe organs. In another large room were stacked large numbers of church organ pipes. Small ones in boxes and some stacked against the walls, several feet long and over a foot across. The last area of the building that I discovered was the repair shop for radiograms, televisions, record players and the like. This workshop had a different atmosphere and different smells, soldering irons and valves. At the end of one lunch break, I returned to the workshop after one of my explorations around the building to find an old straight strung upright piano being moved into the workshop by the porters. The action and keys were missing. Tom was looking over what remained of the instrument when I asked, "What's going to happen to this piano?" Tom replied, "This is for you to start to learn to chip up", "Chip up, what's that?" I asked. Tom replied "It's the term used for doing the early stages of tuning. We do this by plucking the strings". I understood this immediately. It was like tuning my guitar with my plectrum. Tom started counting the notes from the bass end of the piano, every now and then he placed a paper washer on one of the tuning pins. These pins are known as wrest pins. There were several washers all together. Tom said they are just markers for every note to be tuned to C. On all pianos, other than very early instruments, there are three strings to each note, for the top six octaves of the compass. These strings are made of high tensile polished steel. For the bottom two octaves, known as the bass section, the strings have a centre of steel wire and a winding of copper wire wound around at various thicknesses. Tom picked up a tuning lever and a tuning fork for middle C. He then hit the tuning fork on his knee and immediately put the tuning fork between his teeth, placing the tuning lever on the wrest pin at middle C, plucked one of the strings and turned the lever until the string was in tune with the tuning fork. I was mesmerised by this and asked Tom "Why he had put the tuning fork in his mouth?", "Two reasons" he replied. "When I put the tuning fork between my teeth it sends the tone straight to my ear. Not only that, I can hold the tuning lever with one hand and pluck with an ivory plectrum with the other hand". Tom had pulled the first string of the note of middle C into tune. He then placed the tuning lever on the first pin of the next note up which was C sharp. One half semitone higher. He then proceeded to tune the first string of each note all the way to the last note of the piano, checking every octave with the previously marked notes, using the paper washers. He then repeated the process from middle C down through the bass section all the way to bottom C. The bass covered strings came in twos, known as bi-chords, and a half-dozen notes, the thickest strings in all the compass of the piano are just one single string. Tom completed this process in less than ten minutes. He then went to a drawer in his bench and took out an old tuning lever. It had a rosewood handle and a brass collar around the handle of the lever. Tom handed me the lever, it was the same design as Tom's lever, other than the hole in the end was square, whereas Tom's lever had a star shaped hole. Tom explained they do the same job, other than the star shaped hole had eight positions in which it could be connected, and the square shaped lever only had four positions. Tom said, "You can keep the lever as a start of your own kit of tools". "Right, it's your turn. Let's see if you have got the ear for the job". He said, "Place the lever on the second wrest pin down". He then handed me the ivory plectrum and told me to pluck the string. "Can you hear the difference?" Tom asked. I replied "Yes". Trying to tune my guitar at home meant I was familiar with such sounds. Tom told me these are called unisons. All three strings have to sound exactly the same. It was obvious the next string had to come up in pitch to be the same as Tom had tuned. I slowly put pressure on the tuning lever in a clockwise direction, repeating plucking the string, I increased the pressure, and the pins were very tight. I could hear the two notes getting closer and closer until it sounded the same. "How's that?" I asked. Tom replied "Not bad at all. Now pull the third string in tune with the other two". I did as I was told. Tom repeated "Not bad". Now pull the rest of the strings in the same manner. I moved the lever to the next note and repeated the action. "Carry on" said Tom and left me to my task. It took me the rest of the afternoon before I had finished my first encounter with tuning. Tom inspected my effort and said yet again, "Not bad at all for a first attempt".

Over the next couple of weeks, I practised pulling in unisons for not less than one hour a day. My hearing, for what I was listening for, improved. Tom had pointed out the vibrations, as I pulled the string which I was tuning up to meet the string which Tom had previously tuned. As the two strings were plucked simultaneously, they got closer to each other. I had learned to hear the oscillation or vibration. One could hear the *WA, WA, WA*, closer still *WA, WA* until the pure note with no vibration at all. Not only could I hear these pulses, I could begin to feel them through the handle of the tuning lever. Satisfied with my progress, Tom took me to lesson two. He had placed more paper washers on the tuning pins and had written on each one the name of the corresponding note. The whole of the chromatic scale was marked. Tom had chipped up this middle octave between F and F with middle C between the two Fs. I now had to pluck the first notes of the in tune scale and then plucked the octave higher. Just like the unisons, the note had no vibrations when the two became the same, just one octave higher. Over the next few weeks I practised octaves and unisons. My hearing of what I was listening for became clearer and clearer. As I was finishing a session of practising, one Friday afternoon, Tom said that "It was time for my next lesson in tuning".

On the following Monday, just after the morning tea break, Tom told me to go and wash my hands. Tom had cut a new piece of white cotton cloth, the size of a man's handkerchief. Everyone carried a piece of cloth like this in their apron pocket. This was for wiping the keys of any piano after working, tuning or just after having a play. Tom then led the way down the spiral staircase to the first floor, "We're going to the Steinway room" he said. This was a separate showroom solely for Steinway pianos. Tom told me all these pianos are kept meticulously in tune. Tom raised the fall, this is the term used for the name of the lid which covers the keyboard of the piano. The perfect white ivory keys reflected in a mirror image in the shine of the inside of the fall, where, in brass inlaid letters, the name Steinway and Sons was written. Tom sat down at the keyboard. He said "Start at middle C, just like when we are chipping up. It's time for you to learn the sounds of the chromatic scale of equal temperament". Not knowing what Tom was talking about, I said nothing. Without a tuning lever he demonstrated the progression of notes, starting with middle C. While the note of C sustained, Tom played the F below and said, "This is a fifth". He then progressed from C to G and said this was a fourth. With a rhythmic flow, he carried on, using fourths and fifths, until he ended the progression where he started, on middle C. Tom then pulled from his inside jacket pocket a card with the cycle of notes written down. "You're to come down here and play the notes from the card and just listen, and to always wipe the keys with the cotton rag, and never to go in if Mr Fair is in there with a customer".

As instructed, at a convenient time in the day, between doing jobs for Tom, Harry or Albert, I would scuttle down the stairs to the holiest of rooms in the building and go through the progression of notes, listening intensely. I would play the notes in the bass and hear the growl of the strings or go to the treble and hear the pure ping of the notes. I was now starting to realise the differences in various pianos of different makers.

The majority of my time was taken up doing repetitious jobs for Tom and Harry, but occasionally I would spend some hours working with Albert. Albert was a different type of person to Tom and Harry. All three of these men had given service in the Second World War. Albert had been in the merchant navy and I think he must have had a particularly bad time, having survived the sinking of his ship in the North Atlantic. And to make things worse, on his return from the war his wife had run off with another man. On occasion, after afternoon tea, Tom and Harry would sing in two part harmony songs from the First World War. All these songs were romantic and sentimental. "I'll be with you in apple blossom time", "A bicycle made for two" and from the Second World War "There'll be Bluebirds over the White Cliffs of Dover". Only occasionally would Albert join in, with his deep bass voice he completed the harmonious trio. On the occasions that I spent time working with Albert it was a different experience. For Bert would take more time to explain the functions of each component of the workings of the piano. He would set me a task on the rudiments of regulating, this is the term used for adjusting each note, so the hammer hits the strings in the correct manner, so the damper lifted at the right time. At the end of every session of working with Bert, he would whisper to me, "Get out of this trade, you'll never have anything".

At the end of January 1967, I had completed my first six months at Wilson and Peck. Mr Fair delivered our wages on Friday afternoons. On the first pay day in February I opened my pay packet and was surprised, I had my first pay rise, from two pounds and ten shillings to three pounds and five shillings, a rise of fifteen bob. Throughout this period, I had been commuting, by bus or tram, from the red brick suburbs of Sheffield. This was now to alter as my nomadic parents were on the move again.

The new house was a sandstone cottage which was also the Post Office, small shop and tea rooms. Detached and secluded with no neighbours, surrounded by trees on the banks of the river Lyne. The counter for the Post Office, shop and tea rooms were all in one room. It was also our kitchen. At the other side of the counter were two small tables and, on many occasions, I would be eating my breakfast and every chair would be taken by lorry drivers, travelling salesmen and postmen. This location was known as the River Lyne Post Office and Tea Rooms and was the last stop for refreshments before the Snake Pass, the road which crossed the Pennines to Manchester. The river Lyne ran down quite a steep valley, flowing through mature woodland. Wildlife flourished here and the river was full of trout. At the weekends I would explore the valley. Fishing for trout and cooking the best fish of the day. This wild place had not always been so idyllic. Over two hundred years before it was quite an industrial place. Every quarter of a mile or so, were remnants of buildings which were workshops powered by waterwheels. Adjacent, were some small dams. They had been designed so the river water could be diverted via a slush gate. This would keep the water in the dam constant, keeping the waterwheel turning. The men that worked here were silver smiths and were known locally as Little Mesters. I had learnt this, years before at school, studying local history. The Little Mesters crafted silverware and cutlery which made Sheffield famous before it became known as the 'City of Steel'. This haven was my playground and less than five miles to the centre of the city. Being much closer to my work I now commuted daily on my bicycle.

One afternoon, while practising my octaves and unisons, Tom said it was time to learn the next lesson. Demonstrating, he tuned middle C to the tuning fork. He then plucked the G below middle C and pulled the string into tune. "Can you hear that?" Tom asked. "I think so" I replied. Tom then pushed his tuning lever and knocked the note out of tune. "Right, it's your turn" said Tom. I placed my tuning lever in position. Plucked middle C and then G. I turned the pin slowly pulling the string into tune. This was far more difficult to hear than unisons and octaves. "Too sharp, too flat" Tom said. I started to get flustered. For one reason or another I plucked the G first, then the C. This immediately reminded me of the two opening notes of a hit tune at the time by a band called the 'Seekers'. The song was called "The Carnival is Over". Having this sound in my head I tried again to tune the interval called a fourth. This time it was much clearer what I was listening for. Tom said, "That's good, you're learning".

Although I was quite happy in my job, I had taken quite an interest in electronics. This came about from visiting the TV repair shop at the back of the building. There were three engineers and one apprentice who repaired televisions, radios, record players and guitar amplifiers. Albert too, on at least a weekly basis, kept saying, "Get out of this trade, you'll never have anything". Another contributory factor to my thoughts of finding a new job was that whenever I was socialising in the evenings, meeting with my mates, the topic of what we all did for a job cropped up. Many of my friends worked in the steel industry and the girls worked in shops and factories. I soon stopped saying that I was learning to become a piano tuner, as the whole gathering of boys and girls would erupt in laughter at the mention of being a piano tuner. Being of a shy nature I hated the taunting. I started to lie about my new occupation, it was much simpler to say I was an electrician.

On visiting the local labour exchange, I immediately got an interview with a local electronics company called Alfred Peters Limited. At the interview I was told they did not take apprentices for electronics unless one had the relevant GCE's. As I had left school without any of these qualifications, all they could offer me was a job in the sheet metal department, making up the chaises and cases for the electronic components to be mounted on. The hours were eight to five, five days a week, with a wage of five pounds ten shillings. As this was less hours, not having to work Saturday mornings and the wages considerably more, I decided to take the offer. On the following Friday I gave my weeks' notice to Mr Fair and then I told Tom, Harry and Albert. Tom and Harry were saddened of my decision to leave. Tom said, "You showed good promise of becoming a good piano tuner and repairer". Albert said, "Good for you". I worked out my weeks' notice and left the following Friday. Tom, Harry and Albert all shook my hand and wished me luck.

The following Monday I started my new employment. This was a totally different environment to the piano workshop. There were huge machines, guillotines for cutting sheet metal, bending machines and various fly-pressers. I was immediately put to work on one of the latter. I was shown a pile of sheet metal plates, about the size of a playing card. I was to place the first one in a jig on the bed of the machine. Then there was a metal handle on the end of a T bar. On the end of the T bar were two solid balls of metal the size of a football. As one pulled the handle the T bar swung round, this in turn pushed down a punch. The action made a perfect hole in the precise position in the metal plate. This was an easy process. I was left to do pile after pile. The repetition I was used to after the process of 88 after 88 in the piano workshop. It was ironic that tuning pianos was a job using one's ears and that Alfred Peters Limited made audiometers. These machines were made for the health service for testing people's hearing. My time in the metal workshop was not long as my parents had built up the business, improved the property and yet again the property was put up for sale.

THE TRIP DOWN SOUTH

On the day of our move the removal men had nearly finished filling the lorry with furniture when my mother and father had a screaming row. It was all over my mother's rocks. She had always liked unusual stones and other garden artefacts. The removal men had said that there was not enough room on the lorry for her collection, and my mother was not going to leave them behind. To make matters worse my dad appeared to have gone off in the car! About an hour later he returned having bought a sailing boat which was hitched-up to the back of the car. My mother hit the roof, until my father explained his plan. "We'll put some old carpet in the bottom of the boat and then carefully place all my mother's sacred rocks, artefacts and several large potted plants on top!". By midday the removal men had left. Now it was time for my parents to hand over the business to the new proprietors. This would take several hours, having to count all the stock for the shop and tearooms, and then handing over the Post Office keys. While this was going on, I paid my last visit down the river valley.

At the latter end of the afternoon I returned to find the hand-over still not finished. It was almost seven in the evening when we started our journey to Devon. My dad's car was only a mini. I was in the back seat with my guitar and I was not alone. There were our two cats, three Yorkshire Terriers and Polly, a Maltese Terrier. In those days there were virtually no motorways. So, it was the A roads, going from town to town, weaving our way through the counties of England. It was just after dawn, we had passed the Devon County town of Exeter and we were ascending the notorious Haldon Hill. The little mini pulling all the weight up the steep gradient started to over-heat. So, we pulled into a lay-by. We stepped out of the car to stretch our legs and as we looked over the valley, we witnessed the sun rise over the Devon countryside. This beautiful view was to be obliterated within just a few years, by scarring some of nature's finest, with concrete motorways, bridges and underpasses. My dad had re-filled the radiator with water, and we set off on the last leg of our journey. Some two hours later we arrived at Dawn Coppice - the house my mother and I had not seen as my father had bought it on a previous trip to Devon. We entered the short drive; the house was a detached white washed Devon cottage, with a small field, a paddock and two apple and pear orchards. The dogs and cats flew out of the car as soon as the doors were open. We were all exhausted, having taken almost seventeen hours to reach our destination.

A few days later the cottage was coming together - furniture, carpets and curtains, all in their places. I had explored all the land, orchards and outbuildings. One morning after a night of torrential rain, the sun was starting to shine. My dad, having gone outside, to get something from the car, started shouting "Come and look". I went outside, followed by my mother. My father said, "Look at the rain on the car". My mother immediately said, "Oh yes, clean rain". The droplets of water on the car's paint-work were clean. We were all astonished as we were all used to the rain in Sheffield always leaving a black residue over everything it touched. Dawn Coppice was situated between the village of Liverton and the market town of Newton Abbot, three miles away. The following Monday my father started his new position. I was told to go and get a job. After breakfast I cycled to the town of Bovey Tracey where the nearest labour exchange was to be found. I secured a job there and then. No interview, just a phone call. I was to start the following morning, at Dewhurst Butchers, Newton Abbot. This job was to be short-lived. After two or three weeks of chopping up dead animals, one day I severely cut myself on my left hand. As the blood gushed from my wound, the Head butcher said, "Hold it over the steak and kidney". On my return from Newton Abbot Hospital I was told the steak and kidney had sold out early! the Head butcher joked in his broad South Devon accent. I had had seven stitches in my left hand and was not able to work for the rest of the day. I left the butchers shop and went for a walk around the rest of the town. I found myself reading cards on a notice board and I noticed, a neatly written card saying "Young man wanted to assist local builder, doing property maintenance. Good rates of pay. Please telephone". A week later my stitches had been removed and I noticed the card on the notice board was still there. I made a note of the telephone number.

That evening I dialled the number. On answering, a voice spoken in the broadest Devonshire accent "Luscombe Property Maintenance" I replied, "I'm enquiring about the job vacancy" The reply came "Yer not from these parts!" I said "No, I have recently moved from Yorkshire" then he said, "The job was still vacant, and if I was interested, I was to come to his workshop at eight-thirty on Saturday morning". He gave

me the address and I said I would be there prompt. I arrived for the eight-thirty appointment at the given address. I knocked on the door. It was answered by a weather-worn man. He was wearing an old collarless shirt and corduroy trousers, which were supported by, not only a thick leather belt, but also stripy elastic braces. "Can I help you?" he said, I replied "I am here for the job". He asked me into his workshop. On entering the building, he picked up a piece of wood and placed it on his bench. He then told me that he wanted me to measure six inches of wood, mark it and then cut it. I carefully marked, with the set square, and proceeded with his request. He then said, "Could I make a dove tail joint?" I replied, "Yes I could" and proceeded to execute his request. After I had finished my test Mr Luscombe inspected my work. He then said, " The jobs yours if you want it". I replied, "Yes please" and arrangements were made to start the following Monday, after working a week's notice at the butcher's shop. Throughout the summer of sixty-seven I worked for Mr Luscombe, this was very varied work - repairing roofs, replacing windows and repairing window frames which were hand made in Mr Luscombe's workshop.

At the height of the summer there was to be a hippy gathering known as a 'Happening'. This was to take place around a large rock on Dartmoor known as Haytor. A couple of friends I had made in the village asked, "would I like to go?" On the day of the 'Happening' we all met up and started the hike up onto the moor. Along the way we passed a farm where six sisters lived. As we passed the long orchard wall, adjacent to the farmhouse, a voice from nowhere said "Wheres yer goin?" Three of the blonde haired sisters were perched high up in an old apple tree. We replied, "We were going to Haytor to a 'Happening'!" Then the oldest sister said, "Can we come?" The three sisters climbed down the apple tree, shouting to their mother "They're off to Haytor to look at the hippies!" The eldest girl was about seventeen or eighteen. The other two girls were twins around the age of sixteen. They were all very pretty despite being dressed in almost rags and all were barefoot. As our troop walked the Devon lane, leading to the roof of Dartmoor, we all started picking wild flowers. The sisters then plaited flowers and weeds into rings. By the time we arrived at the Tor we all thought we looked like hippies. Nothing much happened at the 'Happening'! A couple of hundred hippy looking people gathered around the rock. There were a few people playing guitars and singing. It was all very innocent and peaceful. After we all bought an ice-cream, we descended all the way down the hill, singing songs of the time - "I looked in the sky where an elephant's eye was looking at me from a bubble gum tree". As autumn came, working for Mr Luscombe was getting very hard. One day I was left to dig the foundations for an extension to a house and was left alone to do this arduous task with wheelbarrow, pick and Devon shovel. I was arriving home so exhausted, my mother asked me if I was happy in my job. I replied, "Not very much", then she asked me "What would you like to do?", my reply was "Out of all the jobs I have done, pianos were my favourite".

BACK TO THOSE 88S

Unbeknown to me, my mother had looked in the Yellow Pages and had found some piano shops. She had picked the nearest, which was in the seaside town of Paignton, and had helpfully telephoned them. She told them about me and that I had worked for Wilson Peck. On my return from work my mum excitedly said, "I have got you an interview at a piano shop.", "where?" I asked, "Paignton" she replied "You've got to be there at half-past nine on Friday". Friday came and I caught the bus to Paignton. My mother had written down the name and address of the company which was Messrs Harris Osbourne Ltd. It was easy to find, being on the main road from Paignton to Torquay. I entered the door and was greeted by an elderly lady. She asked, "Can I help you?" I replied, "I have come for an interview". "Ah, you'll need to see Mr Cotton, come with me young man". I followed the lady to the rear of the shop. She knocked on the door with "Office" written on it. "Come in" was the reply. She opened the door and said, "Mr Cotton, there is a young man to see you", Mr Cotton came out of the office door and shook my hand and said, "Come in and sit down", and I sat opposite him at his desk. "So, you worked for Wilson Peck's?" I replied "Yes". Then he asked me "What I had learned about pianos?" I told him that I had been taught to polish keys, re-centre hammers and of my tuning lessons. Then he said, "Come on, I'll show you around". I followed him into the piano showroom, then into the department that sold guitars, trumpets and saxophones etc etc. I then followed him down a short staircase and through a door into a small room with four easy chairs. This was the tea room and he proceeded to open the next door. I could hear the familiar sounds of pianos being tuned and the smells of French polish and the glue pot. I was then introduced to a man called Fred. He was the workshop foreman. He joined the tour of the rest of the establishment. I was introduced to a lone French polisher; his name was Harry. Mr Cotton opened another door and we were back where we started at Mr Cotton's office. He then asked me if I would like a position. Without hesitation I replied "Yes". He said that he would write to me within a few days. He then led me to the front door of the shop, shook my hand and said goodbye. On my return home my mother asked how I had got on. A few days later a letter arrived addressed to Master Terence Lowe. On the bottom corner of the envelop was the stamp of Messrs Harris Osbourne Ltd. This was a tense moment. I opened the letter and started to read. It said they could offer me a position of apprentice to learn the skills of rebuilding pianos, action-work, regulating, re-stringing and if found suitable fine tuning and toning. The wage they could offer would be six pounds per week and the hours were eight-thirty a.m. to five p.m. Monday to Friday.

A week later I had served my notice with Mr Luscombe. On my last day he dropped me at the gate at the end of our drive. I said "Goodbye" and he wished me luck. As I vaulted the gate I was greeted by my mother. Later on, my mother told me Mr Luscombe had said that I was the best lad he had ever employed.

I started my new job the following week. I was greeted by Mr Cotton and shown down to the workshop. Fred, the workshop Foreman, shook my hand and said to Mr Cotton "Leave him with me John". Fred then said, "Do you smoke?" and offered me one of his cigarettes. We lit up and surveyed a line of pianos in various states of repair. There was a six foot Bechstein grand with its entire insides removed including the iron frame. The sound board had been scraped of its old varnish and was now being rubbed down with sand paper. The next instrument was a Broadwood grand which was further along the process with its freshly gilded iron frame, new red felts and glistening strings. We stubbed our fags out on the floor. "Have you polished keys before?" asked Fred. "Yes", I replied and told him of the process I had learned at Wilson Peck's. "Ah, that's the old fashioned way" said Fred. "This is how we do them here". He led me to a bench with racks of piano keys above it. At the end of the bench was bolted a large electric motor. On the end of the motors shaft was a ten inch across buffing mop. I was familiar with these machines, often peering in backstreet workshops back in Sheffield where women polished the silver cutlery on such buffing machines. Fred switched on the motor, picked up a large lump of brown buffing soap and loaded the mop. He then picked up the first white piano key and held it against the rotating mop, polishing the key one way and then another. He then said, "Your turn". I picked up the next key. On my first attempt, the key flew immediately out of my hands across the workshop. Fred laughed and then showed me what I had done wrong. I soon picked up the knack and was left to make my way through the octaves of awaiting keys.

I was halfway through my task when there were four sharp taps on the central heating pipe. This was the sign to everyone around the building that it was time for the morning tea break. We went into the room with the four easy chairs. "That one's yours" said Fred and pointed to an old chair with wooden arms. I sat down and another man appeared with a tray, with a large tea pot and various mugs, cups and saucers. I was introduced, "This is Fred" said Fred. Fred's job was the repair of violins, general duties and making tea. This small piano shop was a lot more progressive than my previous employment in the trade. I was soon re-stringing my first piano. It was a six-foot Webber grand. Fred taught me how to wind the music wire around the wrest pin, to place it on the corresponding hole in the wrest plank and with a punch and a large hammer beating the wrest pin into the rock elm wrest plank. The job of restringing a piano is not light work and soon my hands had to harden to the task. Mr Cotton had selected an old German upright, on which I was to practise tuning not less than one hour a day. Mr John Cotton was a local man, he had begun learning the piano trade in Devon and as a young man had gone to London and served as an

outside tuner for Broadwood and Sons, piano makers to the Royal Family. Some twenty-five years later he returned to his native Devon. He was a good teacher, explaining the knack of tuning and of setting the wrest pin so the string stayed in tune. I was later to meet the trio of outside tuners who worked for the company. There was Harry, a very jolly man in his fifties. Len, who was in his thirties and finally Mr Hull. Mr Lionel Hull

was a quiet elderly immaculately dressed man, in his three-piece pinstriped suit, white shirt and a full head of silver hair. He was the senior Tuner Technician travelling extensively throughout the West Country maintaining prominent instruments, including the maintenance of the pianos at Dartington College of Arts, and the pianos at Dartington Hall, which included many Steinway grand's, Steinway uprights and various Bechsteins, Blüthners and Bösendorfers, and situated in the Great Hall, the model D Steinway concert grand. Once a year at Easter these pianos were descended upon by the whole tuning staff, headed by Mr Hull. He had looked after the instruments at Dartington from the early days, alongside Leonard and Dorothy Elmhurst, who were the founders of the Dartington Estate. My job was to dismantle every piano, removing the action and keys, vacuuming all the dust and dirt, spraying all the felts with moth proofer. I would replace the keys and then thoroughly clean the ivories and ebony sharps with a cloth and methylated spirits. The action was carefully refitted and finally all the pedal work would be inspected. As I moved to the next piano, Fred, the workshop Foreman would go through the regulation of the action and keys, carefully checking every movement. After this process, one of the tuners would check the pitch of the instrument and tune it accordingly. Finally, the pianos would be checked by Mr Hull. He would execute the final Toning. Toning gives the piano the consistent colour to the sound, the even sound of the piano, pricking each hammer with needles until the desired sound is achieved. Dartington Hall Estate and College of Arts are situated overlooking the river Dart, adjacent to the market town of Totnes. In the Sixties, the town's weekly livestock market was held on a Friday, when all the pubs could stay open all day. This day gave a chance for all sorts of people to descend on the town. On the banks of the river were warehouses full of timber, delivered by ships pulling alongside the town's quay. In the centre of the town was an abattoir where the squealing of pigs could be heard as they were led to slaughter. In the evenings the town would fill up with rockers and greasers on powerful machines, not like the town I know today. Other jobs for the tuners were the pianos in Hotels, Restaurants, Bars and Theatres of Torbay and other seaside towns along the Devon coast.

On one occasion, while assisting Fred, we tuned two pianos in unison. This was done by Fred tuning the first grand piano, in the orchestra pit of the newly built Festival Theatre, situated on the seafront at Paignton. I would then sit and play the notes of the previously tuned piano, while Fred would tune the second piano exactly the same as the first. While striking the desired notes I gazed around the stage of the theatre, looking at pieces of scenery, watching the stage staff preparing for the night's show. As Fred was finishing tuning the second piano, a man appeared, Fred said, "Hello Norman" and they shook hands and I was introduced. Norman was the stage manager of the theatre. On our return to the workshop I said to Fred, "I wonder if there would be any part-time jobs backstage at the theatre". Fred said he would mention it to Norman.

Months passed by in the workshop. My restringing had improved in quality and speed and I was now doing all the re-stringing, scraping and varnishing the sound board and re-gild-ing of the iron frames. This process was to mix up different gold powders to the desired colour, to mix with clear lacquer and then using a spray gun re-gild the plate of the piano. We would undertake the spraying of the iron frames in a lean-too, half out-side in the back yard. One day, as Fred and I were preparing a Bechstein iron frame, Norman, the Theatre Stage Manager, came through the back gates, greeted Fred and said "Terry, if you are interested there is a vacancy for a scene shifter in the evenings". I started my new part-time career half way through the sum-mer show. The stars of the show were Kathy Kirby, the singer and Billy Dainty the comedian. There was a troop of Tiller girls, about sixteen in total. They were supported by six male dan-cers. These summer shows went on for sixteen weeks, twice nightly. My job was to assist a man called Percy. Our job was to stand in the wings and on cue place scenery or strike scenery. This operation had to be carried out mostly in a black-out. On Sundays there would be a change of line up and a visiting show arrived for just one night. Many times, it was Arthur Askey in a one man show. Other times there would be musical evenings. Two of these shows I distinctly remember. There was a band called 'Arrival'. They had a hit called 'Friends'. This band even-tually became one of my favourites, 'Kokomo'. On one of these Sunday shows I was paging one of the tabs, tabs being the name of the big heavy, stage curtains. I was ready for the start of the show. I had my hand on the heavy curtain, Percy on the other curtain. Percy and I would walk in opposite directions, holding on to the heavy curtains. Just before the opening bars of music a guitar headstock hit me in the face, it was not his fault. He prob-ably didn't see me. It was Roy Orbison.

Over the next three years my piano skills improved. As well as the full-time tuning staff, there was one part-time elderly tuner who came in on Thursdays only. His name was Harry. He was the most delightful person and was in his ninety-second year.

Although his suit was a little threadbare, it was freshly pressed for the occasion with his highly polished brown shoes. Being over six-foot-tall, he needed a walking stick, this was also very old – a malaca cane polished with an even more brightly burnished silver handle. Harry's job was to tune some of the stock pianos in the showroom. He would manage three tunings in a day, always leaving enough time in the latter half of the afternoon to come and help me with my tuning. His manner was of a bygone age. He was apprenticed at the age of fourteen with Brimsmead Pianos in London. After he had served his time, he became an outside tuner for the company. Harry reminisced about trips on the train out of London, dressed in a suit, bowler hat and wearing spats around his ankles, he would alight at some rural station and often would be picked-up by pony and trap. It was some time later the thought crossed my mind that Harry was born around the year 1878 and started his life-long career in the piano business in 1892. He was called up and fought in the First World War, survived the Blitz in the Second World War, while tuning pianos in the day and on fire-watch at night. He retired and moved to Devon in the early 1960s. Harry was the most dignified, elegant and patient man. Life and his experiences had polished him as brightly as his shiny shoes.

After the end of the summer season with Kathy Kirby and Billy Dainty there was a two-week rest from the stage work at the theatre. In the autumn it was time for the Torbay Amateur Dramatics Society. This was a week of rehearsals followed by a week of one performance per night plus a matinee on Saturday. This production was Oklahoma. Compared with the professional showman, the excitement and enthusiasm of amateurs combined with the deadly serious pre-madonna's of the leading roles, was quite another experience. After the colourful fortnight of the amateur production there was another rest from the theatre until the beginning of December when it was time for the preparations for the Pantomime season. This show was to be Dick Whittington on ice. In preparation for the ice rink to be assembled, the first six rows of seats had to be removed from the auditorium. Scaffolding was erected over the orchestra pit. The ice engineers arrived and over the following week an ice stage was created. The whole of the stage plus the same again protruding out, passed the proscenium arch. Halfway through December the scenery arrived, followed by the cast. Rehearsals started immediately. I arrived one evening after working on pianos all day to find out I was to be making an appearance. Another stage hand and I were to navigate two ships, mock-up galleons about twelve feet long. We were to get inside a craft, with special hoods that covered our heads and faces. We pushed them around the ice firing cannons at each other. These were flash-bulbs at the bottom of cardboard tubes. Loud music was played with the bangs of the cannon and this was all done in the dark, while the whole scene was lit in ultra-violet, with the mist created by the dry-ice. I never saw this scene but was told it was very effective for Dick Whittington's dream. As well as the main characters there were speciality acts and a chorus of sixteen skaters. Playing the part of Captain Mainbrace was the midget entertainer Kenny Baker. Later on, in his career he was to operate from inside R2D2 for the film Star Wars.

The last summer show I would work for was sixteen weeks of the Black and White Minstrel show. I was to become an assistant Fly-man with Fred who was the Head Fly-man, also John, who was the same age as myself. This show was run like a military exercise, scenes and backdrops had to be changed with precision timing. In one scene, preparations were made behind closed tabs. The compere of the show was doing a few gags. The stage hands had placed together a heart shaped chocolate box. Then I was to fly-down the sparkling heart-shaped lid. There were strict position marks placed on the fly- rope. I would lower the lid to the first mark, the lid would be still vertical, the stage hands then would locate the hinges and place in the hinge pins. Next, I had to fly the lid to the second position, the lid half closed. At this point all twenty or so of the girls in the chorus would have to get in the chocolate box and take up their crouched positions. Then the cue light would tell me to lower the lid to the last mark on the rope. At the opening of the next scene the curtains would open, the Orchestra would start to play. As the lights increased, my job was to slowly raise the rope, opening the chocolate box. At the same time the girls came out dressed as different flavours, singing and dancing. The scene would end with all the chocolates returning to the box and the lid, yet again, had to be closed. After a few weeks into this show, as everyone was relaxing, I relaxed too much and went passed my mark on the rope on the closed position of the chocolate box lid. There were screams from the girls inside. I quickly realised and pulled the rope up to the right position. There was no harm done and the scene opened with no prob-lems, but I got a severe telling-off, not just from Fred, the head Fly-man, then Norman, the Stage Manager and a severe strip-ping down from George Mitchell.

Over the three years or so working for Harris Osborne's, my workload had dramatically increased. On average I was re-stringing an upright or grand piano at one a week as well as re-bushing keys, polishing keys, dismantling actions, replacing springs, loops etc. I was polishing brass work, casters, pedals and hinges, and, of course, practising an hour a day, my tuning. One day, after my tuning session I was teaching myself to play a few chords with a simple melody when Mr Cotton, the Manager, flew through the workshop door. He was in quite a rage and shouting why haven't you been to Palace Avenue. A large grand piano had been sent out on hire to the town's Palace Avenue Theatre. It was for the piano tests and recitals of the collect-ive of local piano teachers. The delivery men had forgotten the hinge pins for the grand piano lid. This being of considerable weight could have severely injured someone if the lid had been raised. It could have slipped off and with no pins to hold it, the force and speed could have caused a severe accident. Mr John Cotton was still ranting and raving when I told him to go and put the pins in himself, "I quit!" I think the tiredness had been building up doing two jobs and I just snapped. Another spoke in the wheel of fate. It was mid-summer. From now on I spent my mornings in bed and my afternoons lying in the sun on south Devon beaches with various girls from the chorus.

LEAVING HOME &
OFF TO LONDON

K nowing that at the end of the summer season of 1970, I would have no job at the theatre. I arranged two days off work and caught the train to London where I could stay with my sister, who had moved to London several months before. I arrived at Paddington station about midday armed with my copy of the A to Z, and my sister's address. I gazed at the map of the London Underground. I had never been to London before, or travelled on an underground train. I knew that I had to get to Ladbrook Grove. After catching the wrong train going the wrong way, more than once, I arrived at my destination. I gathered my bearings and with the aid of my pocket map of London found my way to Latimer Road. I looked up at the decaying terraced house. This area was crumbling. I knocked on the door of the address given. The door was answered by a tall blond women surrounded by at least five young children. "Can I help you?" she enquired. I told her that I was looking for my sister Angela. "Oh yes" she replied "Come in, your sister lives on the top floor, but she's gone out. Would you like a cup of tea?" the blonde lady ushered me to the kitchen, followed by her children. While we drank tea and her children ate biscuits, she spilled out her story. She was born in Austria. At the age of seventeen she had come to London looking for adventure. After meeting and falling for a man from somewhere in Africa she got pregnant and had a baby, followed by six others in quick succession. Then her African husband returned to his country and she was left in the decaying house with her seven children, with no bathroom and only an outside toilet. My sister returned and made an evening meal. Afterwards we looked at the A to Z. I had the address of Broadwood Pianos in Berkeley Square, the nearest underground station being Oxford Circus. The next morning, I walked all the way along Landsdown Avenue to Holland Park Station and caught the Central Line to the West End. Surfacing at Oxford Circus, the cross-roads of Oxford Street and Regents Street, I gazed up at the buildings surrounded by crowds of people. I had never experienced such a scene before. As I walked through the streets of Mayfair there were Rolls Royce and Bentley cars in abundance, mostly driven by peak-capped chauffeurs. As I walked down Conduit Street, I came across Blüthner Pianos and then, across the road on the corner of St Georges Street was Steinway and Sons. I eventually found my way to Broadwood's in the corner of Berkeley Square. I took a deep breath and went through the door. I was greeted by a salesman. I told him I was looking for a job as a piano tuner. The salesman told me to look around while he found someone to see me. I looked around the showroom where there were new Broadwood grand pianos of all sizes along with reconditioned instruments. The salesman returned with a man in a pinstriped suit. I was introduced to him. He was the showroom tuner. Wandering further around the showroom he asked me questions on what I had learnt so far. I was offered a job subject to a tuning test to be arranged at another time. I thanked him very much and returned to the sun-light in Berkeley Square. I walked around with my eyes wide open at the buildings and the people rushing here and there. I found a small backstreet cafe and had a sausage sandwich with a cup of tea. Remembering Blüthner Pianos in Conduit Street, I made my way back there. I looked in the window at the gleaming pianos, all sparkling under the lights from many cut-glass chandeliers. I walked through the door and looked around the various grands and upright pianos. I became spellbound at the quality of the reconditioned instruments. I had never seen such craftsmanship. I had a brief conversation with the showroom manager. He also offered me a position subject to a tuning test. I left Blüthners and gazed across the road at the royal coat of arms above the entrance, above Steinway Hall. I thought, "In for a penny, in for a pound!" I crossed the road and looked up at the coat of arms. It read "By appointment to Her Majesty Queen Elizabeth the Second Pianoforte Manufacturers". I pushed the revolving door into the foyer of Steinway Hall. On the right-hand side were two elderly gentlemen sitting behind a large mahogany desk, with a highly polished brass grill. One of the men, in a foreign accent, said "Can I help you?" I told him I was a piano tuner and looking for a job. Without reply he picked up the telephone and, when it answered, he said "Mr Squibb, there is a young man here says he is a piano tuner and is looking for a job", the man replaced the telephone and told me to take a seat and wait. A short time later, a slight, very well-dressed man came down the grand cascading staircase. He approached me smiling, holding his hand out. I shook his hand and told him my name. He replied, "My name is Squibb, and I am the Manager of Steinway and Sons". He instructed me to follow him to his office. We climbed the stairs to the first floor. We approached a large mahogany door and on it was screwed a brass plate – it read 'Lionel Squibb, Manager'. On entering the large polished office, expensive carpets, ornate mahogany desk and a sole Steinway grand piano, Mr Squibb asked me to sit down on a chair by the side of his desk. He then asked me about what I had learned so far in the piano industry. I reeled off my experiences. Then he asked me what my ambition was. Without a thought I replied, "I'd like your job!" he asked me for my full name and address, and he said that he would write to me in the next few days. That afternoon I caught the train back to Devon. A few days later a letter arrived. On the envelope was Steinway and Sons, London. The letter was addressed to Terence Lowe Esq. I opened the envelope and unfolded the letter. It read "Dear Mr Lowe, we wish to confirm your visit to Steinway Hall today when you made enquiries concerning employment as a piano tuner. As we advised you, we have excellent prospects for piano tuners and technicians, and we would be pleased for you to spend a short time in our workshops before actually beginning a tuning career with us. This would give you an opportunity to check up on any points that may be bothering you, so that you would be really confident. When you have had an opportunity to discuss the matter with your parents, we shall look forward to receiving your confirmation and indication as to when you would be prepared to start. Yours Sincerely Steinway and Sons, L Squibb, Manager".

I was a bit surprised as there had been no confirmation at my interview, no tuning test and further still, how much my wages would be. I wrote back immediately confirming my acceptance of their job offer and I could commence my employment in two weeks' time. The next two weeks I prepared to leave home. I had gathered a small amount of piano tuning tools and had a leatherette attaché case. There was more than one trip to the hardware shop, selecting new wooden handle screwdrivers, three different sizes of pliers and a small hammer. A visit to Burtons bought me my first suit, off the peg, with a free service of taking the trousers up to the right length. Total cost eleven pounds ten shillings. Having written to my sister, I had arranged to rent a small room in the same house in Latimer Road. I left Paignton with an old ex-army suitcase, my tools, my tool box and twenty-five pounds in my pocket. On my arrival at the old crumbling terraced house I was greeted by the Austrian woman still surrounded by her off-spring. She showed me my room, three flights up on the very top floor. This was an attic room, lino on the floor, single bed and an old wardrobe. She said the rent was four pounds a week in advance. I gave her a five-pound note and then with a quick reply, she said that she would keep the other pound as a deposit. I was given my key and the landlady went down the stairs followed by her brood.

The following Monday I arrived at Steinway Hall wearing my new suit, shiny shoes supported by my case of tools. As I entered the building one of the men behind the desk recognised me. He left his chair and introduced himself. "My name is Pesky. I arrange with my colleague all of the tunings". Out of a door, adjacent to Mr Pesky's desk, came a tallish older man. Mr Pesky introduced me. His name was Mr Allen. He was the head salesman. Following Mr Allen, I was taken to the general office to give them my employment cards. On entering, my eyes widened at the original Dickensian desks still being used. The occupants all looking like they were at a church organ, with their matching stools. I was then led to a more familiar environment. This was to meet Steinway's head tuner Bob Glazebrook in his second-floor workshop. I was introduced and while he was chatting to Mr Allen, I looked around at the pianos that were being worked on, old dirty ones, alongside brand new ones.

After Mr Allen left, Mr Glazebrook asked me about what I had learned about pianos so far. He was a man much younger than anyone that I had worked with before. He had a relaxed manner and he soon told me to drop the Mr Glazebrook and said his name was Bob. He then led me to another room where there were several Steinway grands. He selected one which was slightly below concert pitch, and then he said, "Do you think you can raise the pitch?" I replied "Yes". Then I told him that I had never been allowed to practise my tuning on a Steinway before. Bob replied, "That's all you'll be tuning from now on". Bob returned to his workshop and left me to my task. I removed the music desk and propped it against the wall. I opened my tool case and took out my tuning lever, tuning fork and my felt wedgers. I placed a felt wedge between two of the strings corresponding to middle C. I put my tuning lever on the appropriate wrest pin, hit my tuning fork on my kneecap and placed it between my teeth. This sent the sound of the tuning fork straight to my ears. With my two hands free, I could strike the note and turn my crank and hearing the two tones at the same time, pulling the string into tune with the tuning fork. I then moved the felt wedge one string over and then pulled the next string into unison. I carried on tuning fourths and fifths and setting my chromatic scale. It was easier than I had anticipated it would be to tune one of these pianos. The tone was so clear and the tuning pins so smooth, as well as being very tight. After setting my scale of a full octave of notes between F and F and with middle C between the two, I started my ascent of octaves towards the treble end.

Sometime later I heard a voice say, "Want a cup of tea?" I turned around and there was a lad, roughly the same age as myself. "My name's Steven", "My name's Terry", we shook hands. "This way" he said and led me back to Bob's workshop where, on Bob's bench, there were three mugs of tea. Bob was tuning a new Steinway upright. I could not believe the speed with which he was pulling those notes into tune. He was not just playing each note but striking it violently. He tuned the whole treble end of the piano before taking a gulp of tea. He then descended the bass and finished before his tea had gone cold, I was mesmerised. The whole piano tuned in less than half an hour. It had taken me two and a half hours to complete little over two octaves. I spent the rest of the morning finishing my pitch raise.

After lunch, Bob was not to be found in his workshop. I could hear a piano being tuned. I went to explore the source of the sound. I eventually found Steven in another room full of Steinways. Steven told me Bob had gone to the Royal Festival Hall and would be back soon. Steven had only been at Steinways for just over a month and he told me he had previously worked for a company in Oxford, where he came from. On Bob's return he came to inspect my first effort at tuning the Steinway grand. He checked through the intervals and octaves. He then said, "I think we will make a tuner out of you". The next morning Bob handed me one of his old tuning levers (more commonly known in the trade as a 'Crank'). "This is what you need to tune a Steinway" said Bob. This crank was shorter but heavier than my own, with a solid rosewood handle, with a brass collar and the head was threaded, so one could change the size of socket to suit each size of wrest pin. On selecting another grand in the same room, Bob sat at the keyboard. "I heard you tuning yesterday. Fourth and fifths are alright" Bob said, "But a much more accurate way is thirds and sixths, checking with fourths and fifths". Bob proceeded to tune middle C. He then went to E above middle C. This made a major third. Bob enquired "Can you hear the speed of the third?" I replied that I could. He then went to G below middle C, playing the E and the G which made a sixth. Bob pointed out the speed of the vibrations of the C to E, a major third. Then the speed of the sixth, E to G, was so tuned at the same speed as the major third. The next note was B below middle C. This major third was much slower, checking the fourth with the E from the B. It was next E flat above middle C and this third was set slightly slower. Bob then led me to an upright Steinway he had tuned the day before. He showed me the rest of the progression of notes and told me just to play the progression, listening to the speeds of the thirds and sixths. Bob then told me he was off to the Wigmore Hall to tune for a lunch time concert. After Bob's departure I went back to my listening. As I checked the rest of Bob's tuning, his unisons were perfect and so in tune and the perfect octaves, faultless, right up to top C.

I was to spend the next three weeks at Steinway Hall, tuning one piano after another, all day, every day. Bob would often come and give more guidance. He would give Steven and myself tips of what to expect when going out tuning. He told us that most of the professionally used pianos were so well looked after it was probably only the odd unison that would be needed to be attended to. Bob taught me how to set a Steinway in tune so it would stay in tune, from the first chord of a piano concerto to the last. To attain such standards the key must be struck severely hard, almost knocking the string into tune. My tuning exercises became louder and louder, and after a few weeks I could go through a tuning in half the time of my earlier attempts.

The following week I had to report to Steinways Workshops at Park Royal in the suburbs of West London. I was to spend the next two weeks back on the bench. The Workshop Manager was Bob's younger brother Mike Glazebrook and the top technician was a Mr Fred Batson. There were over twenty other men of various ages. I told Mike and Mr Batson what I had previously learned in Devon. For my first task I was given the job of re-stringing a model B. All the hard work had previously been done. The sound board and bridges shone like new under their several coats of varnish. The iron frame had been re-gilded and all the lettering, mentioning the Steinway patents, had been etched out in black. All of the new felts had been positioned and Mr Batson showed me where I could find all the necessary tools and wires and then he left me to it. I wound the first string around the first wrest pin, positioned it in the corresponding hole in the wrest plank. Placed the punch on the pin and struck hard with my hammer. I took my time and made sure every coil was seized tight and every pin driven down to the same height. After a couple of hours. I was just reaching the end of the first section in the treble. All the strings, so far, had been loops. This is when one string becomes two leaving the wrest pin under the "capodastro" bar, across the bridge, around the hitch pin and then back again. The last string was an eye. This is when the music wire is bent around the hitch pin, then held in a pair of pliers and with one's thumb, wound around, completing the making of a single string. Mr Batson then came and inspected my work. He took a careful look, and said "Very neat job, you'll be all right". By the end of the second day I had completed re-placing all the strings on the model B and had chipped it up (the first rough tuning). My finished job was approved by Mike and Mr Batson. The next job I was set to do was to fit a set of hammer heads on a grand action. This particular job I had never done before, so Mr Batson took me through the principles. First of all, reaming the hole in each hammer head to the right size so that it fitted the hammer shank just right. Not too tight and most important not too loose. After all the hammers had been dry-fitted, Mr Batson glued in position the guide hammers. These were the first and last of all four sections. This operation is most critical. The hammers must strike the string at exactly the right point, thus making for the best possible tone. I fitted the rest of the set of hammers and was told my effort was fairly good for a first attempt.

Each night on my return home, I would go straight down to Latimer Road swimming baths. This was not to have a swim but to have a bath, as there was no bathroom in the crumbling terrace. The Victorian white enamel baths were in wooden cubicles with wooden treads on the floor. One could have as much hot water as one wanted. I would fill the bath, which was long enough to almost swim in. On my walk back home, I would look through the open doors of the boiler room, the original Victorian furnace heated enough water for the swimming pool, slipper baths and adjacent laundry. The smell of the coke fired boiler reminded me of the smells of Sheffield.

On my return to Steinway Hall, some two weeks later, I was immediately told I was to go out on my first tuning to tune the piano at the Aeolian Hall. This fine building in Bond Street was originally the show rooms and concert hall of the combined piano makers Aeolian, Steck and Webber and now it was a broadcasting studio, belonging to the BBC. My first mission was a success and there were no complaints. I was then told by Mr Pesky, that I was to meet another Steinway tuner at six am the next morning at the BBC Broadcasting House in Upper Regents Street. I met up with the elderly tuner, prompt, at six am. His name I cannot remember. He introduced me to the men in uniforms on the reception desk, "He's the new boy" the tuner said. "I'm going to show him the ropes". He led me to the lift, where we descended to the lower levels of the bowels of Broadcasting House. There was studio after studio, all with Steinway pianos. The aged tuner had looked after these pianos for years. He told me not to start pulling them about, for he had them all set in tune and most of the time, it was a case of turning up on time and just raising your hat to the piano. The next weeks I was tuning more stock pianos at Steinway Hall, not just older pianos, I was now tuning some of the brand-new instruments situated in the main showroom. This was the largest room in Steinway Hall and was known as the Salon. There was a sea of grands. Lines of concert grands down one side and an assortment of all the other sizes from the smallest grand, the model S, five foot one inches long with a price tag of around one thousand five hundred pounds. The model M, five foot six inches at around seventeen hundred pounds, the next, the model O with a mahogany case, came in at one thousand nine hundred and twenty-four pounds. The model A, six foot two inches in an ebonized finish, came in at just over two thousand pounds. The six-foot eleven inches model B, with a walnut satin case – two thousand four hundred pounds. All of these models came with a choice of case - ebonized dull finish was the cheapest, followed by ebonized high polish. The most expensive was the Sapele mahogany high gloss and the walnut satin closed pore. The remaining larger models came only ebonized dull, or high gloss. These were the model C, seven foot five inches long and finally the model D concert grand at eight foot, ten inches long. Around the walls of the salon were various Steinway uprights.

I was getting more and more guidance from Bob. He explained, by setting the chromatic scale with the thirds beating very much on the fast side, stretching the intervals out as much as one could, this excited the piano, with the thirds beating quickly. If the thirds were on the slow side, this took away the potential of an instrument. Concert pianists from all over the world came in daily and often Mr Pesky was heard conversing in some foreign tongue, for Mr Pesky, as well as doing the tuning arrangements, acted as Steinway's linguist, being fluent in several languages. One day, just prior to lunch, we had a different musician visit Steinway hall. I was tuning down in the basement when Steven came rushing in and in a loud, excited whisper he said, "John Lennon's in the Salon." Like two naughty school boys, the pair of us crept up the rear staircase, which surfaced at the rear of the lift. As we peered around the corner and looking through the lift cage, we saw John Lennon talking to Mr Allen. The pair then entered the senior salesmen's office. Steven and I stayed watching in silence until John came out of the office door followed by Mr Allen. They shook hands and John Lennon left through the front door, accompanied, by what we assume was, his chauffeur. A few moments later the pair of us went to ask Mr Allen if John Lennon had bought a piano. His reply was "Yes, Model B". Mr Allen had just filled out a sold ticket. We followed him into the salon, where he tied the sold ticket to the prop stick of the said piano. Then Mr Allen said in a disapproving voice, "He wants it in white!" The Model B was in a red mahogany case. The piano was to be sent to the workshops at Park Royal. The casework taken to pieces and it was sprayed white.

Bob Glazebrook had not just been coaching me in piano tuning, but also the tuning of the client. All the Steinways on the concert circuit were so well looked after the likelihood of anything going wrong was most remote. Nevertheless, some pianists would make out that there were notes that were not functioning correctly. Bob told me this was probably the case of a nervous performer and the best policy was to take out the action of the piano, check out the offending notes, making out one is adjusting the mechanism, then to slide back the action into the piano and ask the player to try. Almost every time this happened the player would say "Oh yes, much better". Although I had done nothing to the action only pretended to. This was not the case when it came to voicing. This being the process of sticking needles held in a small hand tool, into the felt of the hammers. This operation softened the felt slightly and by going up and down the keyboard, listening to the sound of each note, often a note would sound harder, the action and keys would be pulled out of the piano to reveal the hammers and the offending notes would be pricked on each side of the nose of the hammer. Caution had to be taken as it was not possible to harden the hammer if one pricked too much.

OUTSIDE TUNER FOR STEINWAY & SONS

The next week I was sent to Walthamstow Town Hall where I was to tune the concert grand which was on hire from Steinways. It was for a recording session which featured a soloist pianist accompanied by one of the London Orchestras. I was then to stay all day in case the piano might slightly go out of tune. This was also the way of things for many live concerts at one of the many London concert halls. These sessions were known as tune and attend. After my successful week at Walthamstow I was never to practise tuning at Steinway Hall again, as I was told by Bob that I was ready to go on the road as an outside tuner representing Steinway and Sons.

As I was still living in West London, I would often be given jobs in that area. On my first visit to the Shepherd's Bush T.V. Theatre I had to tune for Carole King. I was standing in the foyer waiting for my tuning card to be signed by the doorman. Carole King came past me in a bit of a strop. As she turned, getting into her chauffeur driven limousine, she said "Thanks for tuning the piano". I was given my work for the week on Wednesdays. This came neatly packaged by Mr Pesky. Each day's work was neatly listed with the pink tuning cards which were for regular clients. We were paid on piece work, the more pianos one tuned, the more one could earn. My first week's earnings came to over twenty-six pounds. I was soon to exceed my income as I gained confidence and experience. I was only too willing for my work load to increase. As my income increased it was time to look for better accommodation. I had heard of a garden flat for rent in Kilburn. I was moving in an upward direction, having a large ground floor sitting room with bay window, a good-sized kitchen with French windows leading to the rear garden and my own bathroom.

An average day's tuning in central London might begin with tunings in various radio broadcast studios for the BBC. As well as Broadcasting House there were studios in Elgin Avenue, Maida Vale or the Golders Green Hippodrome. After these early tunings there would be visits to private houses. I was entering a new world through the front doors of the extremely wealthy. Many were titled people. Around twelve-thirty it would be time to tune at the Albert Hall or the South Bank, the model D Steinway concert grands needing to be ready for the afternoon rehearsals. On some visits to the South Bank I would have to tune the Royal Festival Hall, the Queen Elizabeth Hall and the Purcell room, all in one hour. It was very rare that one would have to attend a rehearsal and a liaison with the pianist after the rehearsal to discuss any problems with the action of the piano or the voicing of the hammers. After which the piano would be retuned, ready for the evening performance. The pianists performing ranged from John Lill, John Ogden, Fou Ts'ong, Daniel Barenboim, Moura Lympany and Andre Previn. One week I was booked to tune and attend a recording session for solo piano. The recording company was Decca and the soloist was Vladimir Ashkenazy. The location was in a building on the Commercial Road in the East End of London. I can remember being nervous of the impending responsibility. On the first day of recording I arrived at least one hour early. I thumped that Steinway into submission. As I had finished laying the scale and had started the treble, the recording engineers had started to arrive. Microphones were placed around the piano and carefully angled to obtain the best sound. I had finished concentrating on the unisons in the treble and had started to descend down the bass when Ashkenazy arrived. He came up beside me and introduced himself. I stood up and shook his hand. I said, "I've almost finished" to which he replied in a most relaxed manner "Take your time" When the last note had been tuned Ashkenazy sat at the piano and started to play. He tried the whole compass of the keyboard. He then paused and said to me, "Very good, but the unisons in the treble are too perfect" He told me he liked the vibrato effect of when the unisons are not quite so true. The sense of relief came over me as the maestro was more than satisfied. There was a relaxed week of making music. The production staff and the soloist were very relaxed and always having a laugh. Everyone called Vladimir, Ashkan!

A similar week's recording was spent at EMI Abbey Road, studio one, with the artist, Andre Previn and one of the London Orchestras. This was when the maestro was with Mia Farrow. She often came in throughout the duration of the recording sessions. Other weeks I would be given tunings in the leafy suburbs: Dulwich, Crystal Palace and Richmond-upon-Thames. In the autumn of 1970, Edward Heath had become Prime Minister and one of the first things he moved into number 10 Downing Street was his Steinway grand piano. This was pictured on the front page of the quarterly edition of the Steinway news. On delivery of the model A Steinway, Bob Glazebrook had been booked to tune the piano, on arrival at number 10.

Going into the various studios, theatres and concert halls was now an everyday occurrence, to which I felt quite at home. The years I had spent as a stage hand had paid off, as I was not fazed at being in the company of famous names, whereas one new tuner had gone to pieces and was never sent to such a venue again and instead he was to become a suburban tuner. At the end of 1970 in December was the Steinway and Sons annual dinner, to which I still have a copy of the menu; hors d'oeuvres, halibut bon femme followed by chicken chasseur and then cassata. This was accompanied by a selection of different wines. The whole of Steinway's staff from Steinway Hall, the workshops at Park Royal and many outside tuners and technicians that I had not yet met. These members of staff covered various areas of the provinces. On this particular occasion Henry Z Steinway, then the head of the Steinway Dynasty, flew from New York for the occasion. He gave a speech and then presented Mr John Allen with a small red badge to commemorate, and thank him for, fifty years' service for Steinway and Sons. I can remember thinking I would like more than a little red badge for fifty years work. It was shortly after the annual dinner that the Steinway family sold Steinway and Sons to the media company CBS.

Although I had always taken pride in my appearance, I now had three new quality suits and several pairs of good shoes. Even so on one visit to Steinway Hall, Mr Squibb abruptly said to me, "Lowe, fingernails!" I immediately held out both my hands like a naughty school boy. The Steinway Manager inspected each hand carefully and said "Good, good", smiled and carried on his way. In the New Year of 1971 there was talk of me acquiring a car. The policy in those days was for each outside tuner to buy his own car and then to claim back petrol and expenses. If necessary, the company would advance a loan to buy the vehicle which would then be repaid weekly out of one's wages. I had been looking around at second hand cars and had been attracted to a MG Midget. I reported this to Mr Squibb. He said that such a car was not the right image for the company. A couple of weeks later I was told the company had decided to start and buy outside tuners a car and I was to have the first. I was told by Mr Pesky that everything had been arranged and I was to collect my new car from Kennings, Regents Park. After a full work load on the last day of the week I arrived at Kennings at around 4.30 pm in the afternoon. I entered the showroom. I was greeted by a salesman. I told him I was from Steinways and was here to collect my new car. His reply was "It's all ready". He led me to a side door out of the building and there was my brand new Mini 1000. It was light brown with red seats. The salesman handed me two sets of keys, I signed his papers and I was on my way. I got behind the wheel. I was excited and nervous. I had learnt to get around London on public transport but had not a clue about driving around the capital. I had to be at the Royal Festival Hall for a tuning at 6pm. It was quarter-past six when I was crossing the River Thames on Waterloo Bridge and looking down, I could see the South Bank. I was getting swept away by the rush hour traffic and found myself halfway down the Old Kent Road on the way to Lewisham before I managed to turn around. I was late for my tuning and had to go through my job with the whole of the London Symphony Orchestra around me. The string players - violins, violas, cellos, double basses - all tuning their instruments, the trumpets, horns and trombones warming up and the harpist, plucking and tuning, and the audience arriving and taking their places in the auditorium. After I had finished, I had to attend the first half of the concert. I took refuge in the artist's bar with a hot pot of tea.

My new car was liberating. No more tubes and buses. My work pattern immediately altered. I was sent much further afield. The next Monday I was sent to Marlborough, Wiltshire. I checked in at a local hotel in the centre of the town, as I had three days' work and then, at ten o'clock reported to the office of Marlborough College. There were several grand and upright pianos to tune, as well as several private residences' around the area. By the end of the week I was back in the West End. As well as countless musical venues around town, there were also the pianos in hotels. A particular pleasant morning's work was to start at Grosvenor House in Park Lane. After which it was the Dorchester, the Hilton, finishing with the Bunny Club. The Savoy Hotel, in the Strand, had a Steinway grand which had a small brass plaque which read, "This piano was played by Carole Gibbons for live broadcasts by the BBC during World War 2".

There were tunings in gentleman's clubs; the reform club, the constitutional and the savage club etc, etc. One thing these places had in common was the smell. If the tuning was anywhere near lunch time, the aroma of school dinners wafted in the air. Not the school dinners I had known, but the smell of school dinners like at Marlborough, Eton and Harrow. One visit to Stowe school was to tune a model D on hire from the Hall which had been chosen for a recital by Alfred Brendel. I can remember tuning the concert grand and gazing out of the window at the huge open spaces covered in rugby pitches. This was a far cry from the Victorian school house I had attended, with its tarmac playground and outside lavatories. I had tuned for Alfred Brendel on previous occasions and knew he was more bothered about the evenness of the voicings of the piano than that of the tuning. I had finished tuning when the soloist arrived. I had removed the fall, key-blocks and lock front ready for the Maestro to try. He would go up and down the keyboard playing each note chromatically. Then he would stop and say, "A little off that one". I then would withdraw the action and slightly needle the corresponding hammer. This process was repeated many, many times. Alfred Brendel often used to wear plasters on his fingers.

There were many Stately Homes I visited, amongst them, St Pauls Walden Bury in Hertfordshire. This was the home of the Bowes-Lyon family. Several silver framed photographs of the Royal Family were displayed on the top of the grand piano. One in particular I remember was of the Queen Mother admiring roses in the garden. At this out of the way mansion, on one visit the butler entered the room where I was tuning. He asked me if I would like lunch. At the same time, I was being sniffed around the ankles by a quartet of dogs. This, I presume was the Royal Corgis. There were visits to Kensington Palace, St James Palace and Windsor Castle. A regular tuning down in the New Forest was for two brothers of the Rothschild family. One brother had two concert grands placed together. One a Steinway and the other a Blüthner. Both pianos had to be tuned in unison. This house was a very modern mansion. The older brother, The Baron De Rothschild, lived a few miles away in a traditional stately home. This was like going back in time. There was a full-staff of servants, gardeners, chauffeur and the head butler. I had joined all of them on one visit for afternoon tea. I had tuned the Steinway in one of the vast drawing rooms, after which I was led by the butler to the staff room. There were wooden tables with school-like wooden chairs to sit on. There was a large tea pot on each table along with several plates of bread and jam. After one visit I had left and having driven along the south coast to Chichester. Here I was to tune the Steinway at the Theatre in the Round. This was for the accompanist who played for Rostrop-ovich, the world-renowned cellist.

After a day tuning around the Croydon area, which always in-cluded the Selsdon Park Hotel, the last tuning of the day was usually at Fairfield Halls. One such visit was tuning for Semp-rini at the piano, accompanied by the BBC Concert Orchestra and the show was a live broadcast for 'Friday Night is Music Night'. I can remember turning on my car radio and listening to the notes coming out of the Steinway at the hands of the great showman Semprini. On the many times I had tuned for Semp-rini, I can never remember seeing any sheet music. I think he had memorized all the popular classics. On one particular tune and attend I had arranged to meet a girl. After giving the con-cert grand my full attention I made my way to the foyer to make my rendezvous, on route I had called into the booking office and asked if there was any chance of a couple of seats. I was in-formed it was a full house. I met my date and informed her that unfortunately there were no vacant seats and as I was to attend the concert, we would have to go behind the concert platform and listen from there. We found a place to sit but without a view of the orchestra. At that point one of the stage staff asked, "Had I not asked the booking office for two seats out front?" I told him that it was a full house. He said "Wait a minute ". He promptly returned and told us to follow him. I asked him where we were going. He said, "I've got you two seats". He opened the door. As we went through, we were greeted with a view overlooking the orchestra and the whole of the auditorium. It was the Royal Box. We sat down feeling rather self-conscious. The first half of the concert included a piano concerto. The second half of the evening was a performance of Tchaikovsky's 1812. At the point in the Overture where the canons are fired, this particular performance, unbeknown to me, was using real canons. As the thunderous noise played its part, simultaneously the whole of the Royal Box was consumed with clouds of smoke. We could not see the orchestra. As the smoke cleared, the feeling of self-consciousness was overwhelming, as there seemed to be more smiling eyes focused upon us than there were on the orchestra. The stage staff had had their laugh. It was my first and last date.

Some weekends the workload was even greater. One particular Sunday started at Decca studios, West Hampstead. In one studio full of rock instruments was the Moody Blues. I then had a tuning a Maida Vale BBC after which the BBC Concert Hall, Broadcasting House, then the Albert Hall and finally, the Royal Festival Hall. All these instruments had to be in tune by no later than 1pm. In the afternoon there was the Purcell room piano and the Queen Elizabeth Hall. After a short break, and after the afternoon rehearsal, I returned to the Festival hall piano and then a dash across London to the Albert Hall, just in time to check the tuning for the evening performance.

One Sunday the last tuning in the afternoon was at the Rainbow. I arrived around 4pm. The "All American Band" was playing; trumpets, trombones, saxophones and a full rhythm section; bass, drums, two guitars and in the centre of the stage, the Steinway grand piano. The orchestra wound down. I was asked to tune the piano as quickly as possible. As I was tuning, my gaze went past the end of the piano and there was Peter Sellers sitting on a chair in the wings, immaculately dressed, and sporting a deep sun tan. His charisma radiated. As I finished my tuning, I tested my work with some simple jazz chords which I had been learning, when, from behind me came singing and dancing Liza Minnelli. She was improvising to the notes which I played. Not knowing what to do, I repeated my chord progression to which Liza repeated her verse. There was a roll on the drums and the impromptu moment was over. Liza Minnelli thanked me for tuning the piano and said to keep learning the chords.

When tuning in the South London area, there was one piano I regularly had to attend. The Steinway grand was situated in the centre of a ward, in the Home for Incurables. While tuning the grand I would peer around at the bed ridden people who were never going to recover from their illnesses. As I tuned the notes there would be the moans and groans and occasional screams of people dying in pain. One would feel grateful to be alive and well after finishing that job.

On a visit to Steinway Hall to pick up my wage cheque and the next week's work, I bumped into Steven. He to, was now tuning full time, visiting the same venues as myself. We managed to find the time to have lunch together. Steven told me that he had been given the follow-up tuning to John Lennon's, now, white piano. He told me the delivery crew had to wheel-in the instrument into the house at Virginia Water, in silence. The reason was that Yoko Ono was sleeping and the piano was a present to her. After the Steinway removal team had left, Steven had helped John Lennon to rap a pink ribbon tied in a bow around the piano. Steven had then had to wait until Yoko Ono had risen. After Yoko Ono was presented with her gift Steven then carried out his tuning. I can remember feeling envious of Steven for landing that job. It was the spring of 1971 and the world-renowned pianist Artur Rubinstein was in town. Bob Glazebrook was tuning for all his concerts, but I was given the tuning of the Model K upright Steinway which was located in the soloist's dressing room, in the Royal Festival Hall. Unfortunately, I never met the great man.

One visit to EMI studios, Abbey Road, I had to tune the Steinway for Pink Floyd. The studio was full of instruments and a drum kit covered in microphones. Then I had to tune the upright Steinway kept in the corner of studio two. This studio was the studio where the Beatles had recorded most of their music. The tuning of this particular Steinway upright was a different process to the norm. The piano was first put perfectly in tune and then one of the three unisons was tuned slightly flat. This was done to every note carefully making sure the flattened string was tuned the same amount on each note. This was known as a Jangle piano, tuned honky-tonk. The recording session was for the one and only Mrs Mills. Another studio I regularly visited was Dick James Music, New Oxford Street. Although I never met Dick James, I was impressed with him as he had sung the theme tune from my favourite T.V programme from when I was a young boy "Robin Hood".

As the summer arrived, the proms started at the Albert Hall and I was to tune there almost daily. By the end of the summer I had two pairs of shoes where only the right-hand shoe, of each pair, had developed holes in the soles. This was from the amount of brake and accelerator action, from the miles of driving in and around the capital. A regular tuning of one of the smaller concert hall venues was the Wigmore Hall. Tuning's were often for lunchtime concerts. On emerging back on the pavement on Wigmore Street, I would often peer into the window next door, which was Bösendorfer Pianos. After one such visit, I decided to enter the showroom of Bösendorfers. I walked around the cluster of various sized grands. As I was looking into the insides of one of the largest grand's, a voice said," Michael Marney, can I help you?" I introduced myself and told him that I was a tuner for Steinways, and that I was interested in having a look at the largest grand piano in the world – The Bösendorfer Imperial. Michael Marney then sat down at the nine-foot monster and started to play. He played exceedingly well, starting with Rachmaninov and then he would metamorhpose, through improvisation, into Ravel and finally finishing with some Chopin. The sound of the piano was overwhelming, not better or worse than a Steinway, but different. I was on a tight schedule as normal, so thanked him for the demonstration. He replied, "Call in anytime".

After the 1971 Proms, at the Albert Hall, where I had been almost on a daily basis for various concerts, it was a welcome change to return to Hampshire and the New Forest. Steinway's policy for a domestic tuning was not for less than four tunings per annum. By now, I could find my way to the more hidden addresses without having to ask at the local Post Office, or by asking strangers en route. I had, so far, not had any serious comebacks or complaints regarding my standard of work. At some point every tuner's name came up on the tuning cards that they were not to visit certain clients. We were told by Mr Pesky not to take it personally if one's name appeared. Sometimes your face just doesn't fit. The first time my name appeared "Not Lowe", was not to be repeated. Lowering the pitch of an instrument! This occurred when tuning a Steinway model K upright, at an address in Dulwich. When checking the pitch with my tuning fork, I found the pitch was way too sharp although the instrument was within reasonable tune within its self. I decided to lower the pitch to the correct A 440. In all the time I had been tuning I had never lowered the pitch, only raised it. When the pitch is raised, a piano reacts afterwards by going out of tune, but usually a second tuning will rectify the problem. When a piano is lowered in pitch, the whole of the instrument becomes unsettled and it can take several tunings before it settles down again. I was put on the carpet by Bob when the complaint came in. I told Bob that I had lowered the pitch on the Model K. Bob, in his mellow manner, gave me the advice, "If at all possible, never lower the pitch as this action upsets any stringed instrument far more so than when the pitch is raised".

Tuning around the capital, I had visited just about every venue a piano could be found in. I was now familiar with most of the commissionaires, doormen and security people. Towards December 1971 the real busy period of the year had started. People getting their pianos tuned for Christmas and, many weeks before the end of the year, the Christmas television and radio shows were recorded well in advance. One such a tuning was at the BBC Television Centre. On the tuning slip it read, 'The artist is Andre Previn'. As I entered TC8, Eric Morecombe was coming out. He was wearing a Deer Stalkers hat and smoking a larger than life Briar pipe. I tuned the concert grand and just left the studios as everyone had gone to lunch and there was no sign of Andre Previn. When I saw the programme on television I could not stop laughing and could not believe how Andre Previn kept a straight face throughout the sketch, which was hysterical.

As I was driving and tuning all the time, I started to miss working on the bench, and not only this, I was missing working on other makes of pianos. After another lunchtime tuning at the Wigmore Hall, I revisited Michael Marney at Bösendorfers. As we chatted, over a cup of tea, he informed me business was picking up and that Decca records and in particular Argo records were starting to hire Bösendorfers for their recording sessions. I jokingly said, "If you ever need a tuner, let me know" His reply was to ask for my address. A week later I received a letter from Marney saying Bösendorfers have the pleasure of offering me the appointment of "Tuner Technician".

Over the well-earned Christmas break I pondered Bösendorfer's job offer. I then thought about the two years I had been on the road, the thousands of miles I had driven, the people I had met and the number of Steinway pianos I had tuned. In the letter from Bösendorfer's, Marney mentioned that we could build up the business, for as well as tuning, the basement of 38 Wigmore

Street could be used as a workshop for the repair and restoration of all makes of pianos. The thought of working at a bench, with my apron on, tipped the balance. In the New Year of 1972, I gave my notice to Steinways. Mr Pesky was so surprised and said he regretted me leaving. John Allen said, "Are you sure you want to leave, you have a good future here." My answer was "Yes". I was about to start an association with 38 Wigmore Street which would last for several happy years.

38 WIGMORE STREET

As I was in the habit of rising early, it was just after 8am when I surfaced from the underground at Oxford Circus. My new Prince of Wales checked three-piece suit, white shirt and blue tie. My latest tool bag was an old doctor's Gladstone bag. I had polished the brown leather case at the same time as I had polished my shoes. On my walk across Cavendish Square, I happened to notice the first building on Wigmore Street had on its walls a motif of cupids, all playing musical instruments and in the centre of the frieze was a grand piano. Wigmore Street, a short distance north and running east to west, parallel to Oxford Street, here the atmosphere was different to the glitz of Mayfair, where I had served with Steinways. Adjacent to Wigmore Street ran Harley Street and Wellbeck Street, where the medical professions held their establishments. After having breakfast in a small cafe in Marylebone Lane, I walked towards Bösendorfers. I had noticed many small businesses below street level, in various basement workshops there were hat makers, furriers, tailors, hairdressers and jewellery makers. Just before 10am I entered 38 Wigmore Street, my first day with Bösendorfers. Michael Marney was sitting in his office. I knocked on the door, entered and was greeted by Michael "Ready for a cup of tea?" he said. This was a new situation for both of us, unlike at Steinways with its army of tuners and workshops, full of technicians. Here it was Michael, the manager and now, me, the sole tuner and technician. There was no ready tuning round, just a stock of various Bösendorfer grands, ranging from the smallest to the largest. I suggested to Michael that I would start and tune all the stock of instruments, beginning with the Imperial 9'6" concert grand. On closer inspection, I decided to give the instruments a good clean. The cases were kept shiny and dust free, but the strings, iron frame and the sound board were matt finished with dust. I spent most of the morning on the Imperial. In the afternoon the 9' concert grand got the same treatment, followed by the 7'4". This model of Bösendorfer was to become my favourite.

Also situated on the ground floor, at their desks, were two receptionists, who ran Wigmore Studios. On the upper floors there were approximately a dozen rooms all with a piano. Some rooms with an upright but the majority with a grand. The studios were for rent on a weekly, daily or hourly basis. Some studios were used by piano teachers, others by singing teachers. One room was used by Glynis Johns the actress, where she gave elocution lessons. Over the next few days while sitting and tuning, I observed a constant stream of people going in and out. As well as the studios there were many offices for various individuals. One person, who was unmistakable for his tall stature, was Sir Adrian Boult, the eminent conductor. Passing me on the way to the lift, he recognized me as I had tuned several times before when Sir Adrian was conducting. He said, "Hello sonny, come over to the opposition?" As well as Sir Adrian's office, there was the violinist Yehudi Menuhin and Arthur Owen, who was an agent for opera singers and the musical publication company, 'Patterson's'. By the end of the week the stock of Bösendorfer grands were all gleaming and in tune. The next week a deal was done with Wigmore Studios and I was to work my way through tuning and improving the overworked pianos. There were several different makes of instrument; Becksteins, Petroffs and Blüthners. A number of the Bechsteins had been there for decades. 38 Wigmore Street and Wigmore Hall, next door, were originally one and the same, Bechstein Hall. While working on one of the studio pianos, Marney came through the door and in an excited voice said, "I have just sold a model 6'8" to London Weekend Television. The television company had just built a new studio complex on the South Bank and the new Bösendorfer was to be delivered by the end of the week. I was to go along and tune it as soon as the delivery men had assembled it. Michael then said he had got confirmation of a week's hire of the Imperial concert grand. The instrument was to go to St John Smith's Square for Argo Records, and the soloist was John Ogden. I was to tune and attend for the whole week's recording session. On the following Friday the new instrument was delivered to London Weekend Television in its bright mahogany case and was already assembled by 10am. While I was tuning, a member of the administration staff introduced herself, she asked "Could you tune the piano on a regular basis?" I replied, "Of course, just make all the arrangements with the office". By the time I had returned to Wigmore Street, Michael had been called by the lady from London Weekend Television. I was to tune the piano on a weekly basis. The piano was to be tuned by 10am on Monday mornings. Other tunings were to be arranged prior to live broadcasts. Harry Rabinowitz was the musical director for the television company. He would conduct a small orchestra for such programmes as the Russell Harty Show and the Reg Varney Show. The small orchestras were made up of various session musicians and always played live for each occasion. The week of the recording sessions at Smith's Square were like a working week, starting at 10am. I would arrive before 9am, tuning the Imperial, ready for a 10am start. St John Smith's Square had been restored after taking damage in the Second World War. The Baroque style church, being just a short walk from the Houses of Parliament, was renowned for its particularly good acoustics. The rear of the old church, in a separate room, was filled with the recording equipment; a pair of large loudspeakers, a recording desk and two tape recorders. The producer was Bob Auger. The recording engineer was Stan and the tape operator, a young man of roughly the same age as me. A music student from one of the London music colleges was also employed, to sit next to John Ogden and read along the music as it was played and at the precise time, turn the page over. One morning, the page turner failed to turn up and the producer asked if I could do the job. I explained that my reading of music was limited, but that I would "Have-a-go". I sat next to John Ogden and told him of my limitations reading the musical stave. He reassured me and told me he would give me a nod at the right time. The corner of the page was bent over ready for a quick turn. The instruction from the producer came through a talk back speaker, wired from the control room. As the virtuoso started to play, I tried to keep up and soon realized that I was totally out of my depth, so I just kept an eye on John's face. I saw him raise his head; at that point I placed my fingers on the pre bent corner and turned the page over. John carried on playing. John and myself managed our situation for the rest of the morning, when, to my relief, the music student arrived just before lunch.

Bösendorfers 38 Wigmore St 1973

Bösendorfers, at this time, were the only competition for Steinways and they were starting to get busier. Regular hirings to the main concert halls, recording studios and television studios, and sales were picking up. Roger Woodward, the acclaimed Australian pianist, had purchased an Imperial concert grand. On regular visits to his house in Knightsbridge, I noticed that Roger had made a bed up, under the piano, where he could occasionally be found having forty-winks, after intense sessions of pounding the monster Imperial.

Another sale of a model 7'4" was made to Pete Townshend of The Who. The piano was delivered to his house in Twickenham. One day I was tuning in the window of 38 Wigmore Street when a huge motorcycle stopped outside. The leather clad rider gave a final rev of his deafening machine and dismounted. On entering the building, he took off his helmet revealing his long hair, the two ladies on reception looked in amazement, with a hint of fear. The character approached me and asked if he could try the pianos. I told him to try any of them. The two ladies peered-on, their jaws almost dropping in unison. The most beautiful melodic music filled the showroom. I later found out the music being played was Haydn. This I didn't know, but I had recognised the leather clad man, it was Keith Emerson.

Although the work was increasing, there was still not the amount that I was used to at Steinways. Meanwhile, I had become friendly with the company of movers, who handled all the deliveries of pianos, called Piano Transport, a private concern. PTS, as they were more commonly known, was co-owned by Fred and McGuinty. Also, there was Terry and Fred's young son David. Fred was a veteran of the Second World War. Fred had a claim to fame, for after a difficult delivery of an upright piano, up a rather tight staircase, a song had been written of the saga. The piano was for Bernard Cribbens and the song was called "Right said Fred". I had asked Fred if he knew of any private work. He gave me a number of a piano teacher who lived in Elgin Avenue, Maida Vale. Fred told me she was doing a bit of buying and selling. The name of the teacher was Reva Gordon. One evening I telephoned Mrs. Gordon, I told her I was a tuner and was looking for extra work. She told me her address and said come round.

any time. The next evening, I had free, so I went to Elgin Avenue. I rang the bell and over the intercom a voice said, "Yes, who is it?" I replied, "Mrs Gordon, its Terry the Piano Tuner". Almost straight away, the door opened, "Hello, hello, I am Reva" she said. We shook hands and I followed her into the entrance hall and through the front door to her ground floor flat. I noticed, as she went through the door, she almost touched each side of the door jam, for Reva Gordon was not only a larger than life personality, she was also very, very large and wore dresses like Demis Roussos. The vast sitting room, with its high ceilings, baronial fireplace and alcoves on either side, each with a grand piano. Along one wall stood four upright pianos of various sizes. Reva poured me a glass of wine. I sat down in an armchair. Reva sat at one of the grand pianos and started to play. She played extremely well. "What would you like to hear?" she asked. I replied "Claire de Lune". Immediately her hands hit the first notes of Debussy's masterpiece, playing the whole work through. Reva then told me "This is my beautiful Broadwood. I had Mr. Batson, from Steinway's, fit new hammers and regulate the action. It was over two years that he did the work and it is still beautiful to play". I told her that I knew Fred Batson from when I had worked in Steinway's workshop. Reva finished playing and told me she had been teaching piano for ten years. Six months ago, she was given an upright piano from one of her students, but having been delivered, she decided she didn't really want it. So, after having it tuned, she placed an advertisement in the Ham and High, the Hampstead and Highgate local paper. She proceeded to tell me that the phone never stopped ringing and she could have sold it several times over. Being impressed by the response to the ad, she then told me that she found two cheap upright pianos and had her elderly piano tuner, a man called Mr White, from Crystal Palace, to go through the tuning and regulation. The advertisement in the newspaper was repeated. The two pianos were sold the very next day. Reva poured another glass of wine. She then told me the profit on the two pianos was as much as a month's income from teaching. Shrieking with laughter, she said "So now I teach the piano and also buy and sell them!"

I started tuning and repairing pianos for Reva Gordon in her mansion flat. This I managed a couple of evenings a week. These visits always ended with food being served. Slowly, different people would arrive, the wine flowed, there was some extremely talented musicians taking turns to play their pieces. Reva's husband occasionally popped in, he was a scientist doing research into things he could not talk about, having signed the Official Secrets Act. He got on very well with Riva's friend and lover, a tiny skinny African man, with an unpronounceable name. I looked forward to my visits to Elgin Avenue. I got paid in cash for my work, was fed with extremely good food and wine and I enjoyed, very much, the bohemian environment.

UP GOES THE TEMPO

By the end of 1973 the sales of Bösendorfers' were dramatically increasing; also, many pianists were hiring Bosendofers for concerts, recording sessions and recitals. Sometimes, I could not cover all of the tunings, so Michael would call for the services of Mr. Lionel Box. Mr. Box, as I addressed him, was well over retirement age, he had a smiley round face and was always immaculately dressed, in a three-piece pinstriped suit, white shirt, with a polka dot tie and finished off with his bowler hat. Another technician was called in, Les Pearce. He was a tall man, in his forties, and had done his apprenticeship with Challens, just after the war. He and his brother, who was a first-class French polisher, ran their piano restoring business, located in two old prefabs in Kentish Town. Les had a no-nonsense attitude to pianos. Les, being a first-class craftsman, would attend to the regulation of the actions of the higher pianos. Between Les and myself, we honed up the hire fleet.

Visiting players had favourite instruments. Oscar Peterson was making regular visits to England. I tuned and attended many engagements at the Albert Hall, the South Bank and Ronnie Scott's. He always greeted me with a big handshake and an even bigger smile and would say "How ya' doin' Terry". On one of Oscar Peterson's visits, I was tuning his favourite Imperial Bösendorfer, in studio 8 at the BBC television centre, and he was joined by the jazz violinist Stephan Grappelli. I stayed for the show; the experience was a piece of musical genius, as improvising together was an effortless exercise for both of them. Another jazz player who was using Bösendorfers was Jacques Loussier, playing versions of Bach, delivered in his distinctive jazz style. For one of the concerts at the Albert Hall, instead of playing one of the concert grands, he had chosen the 7'4" model. I think he had made an interesting choice, performing with just a double bass player and drummer, the balance of the trio was just right. There were recording sessions at St John Smith's Square, again for Argo records. This time I had to tune two Imperial concert grands, having to have them ready and in tune for a 10am start. It was an early start, and after I had finished the first tuning, I asked the tape operator to play various notes of the in-tune piano so I could have reference, so the pair of Imperials were exactly in unison, note for note. The performer, again John Ogden was this time joined by the accomplished pianist, Brenda Lucas, his wife. The music which was to be recorded over the next several days was Liszt and Schumann.

Every so often there was an occasion with a difference. One such event was a gala evening promoting various keyboards. This was to be held at the Tunbridge Wells Assembly Halls. The Bösendorfer Imperial was to be the highlight of the evening and the pianist, to show it off, was Semprini. Michael Marney, his wife and I, had driven from London on the morning of the "Spectacular". On our arrival at the Assembly Hall, we were greeted by an array of keyboards, electric organs, harpsichords and spinets. Michael his wife and Semprini all went out to lunch. I was told by Michael not to leave the Imperial and not to let anyone attempt to play it. There were other tuners, tuning and tinkering with their instruments. It was not until four in the afternoon that it was my time to execute my tuning. By the time I had finished, it was almost time for the beginning of the programme. I told Michael everything was fine and I was going out for something to eat. Michael said I had better not leave the vicinity and he would try and get me a sandwich. The first half of the evening started with pieces of music played on the harp-sichords. While this was going on I had somehow found myself in the company of Reggie Dickson. He was famous for playing the organ at the Blackpool Tower Ballroom. He was going to start the second half of the event, demonstrating a new, very large, electric organ. We spent the next hour chatting in his dressing room. I was now extremely hungry; no sandwich had turned up from Michael. Reggie had taken the top off a bottle of whiskey, he also produced a large bag of salted peanuts, which he told me to help myself to. I started devouring peanuts, washed down with whiskey. Semprini finished of the evening with a standing ovation. On the way back to London I was sit-ting in the back of the Ford Cortina estate. Michael and his wife chatting in the front. It was after midnight and very little traffic was on the road. Michael was driving quite fast, I was being tossed left and right around every traffic island, which there were any amount of, on the old roads. Michael was puffing away on his awful smelling pipe. Michael's wife did not want any of the windows open. By the time we were passing through Lewisham, the peanuts, mixed with the whiskey, and inhaling the acrid pipe smoke, and being tossed around like a rag doll, I started to feel quite sick. I asked Michael to stop the car. I got out and found somewhere discreet to throw up. I can remember holding on to my new silk tie so as not to cover it with vomit. I turned round to go back to the car, there was no car, just my tun-ing bag left on the pavement. Here I was stuck in South London and there was no one around. Luckily I found a private hire car willing to take me home to North London. The next morning Michael Marney said that I had blotted my copy book. At this accusation my blood went up and I raised my voice and told him "Next time you want a tuner to sit around all day and night, without refreshment, find someone else". Michael backed down and apologised for forgetting to get me a sandwich, he also re-funded me my Taxi fare and asked if I had got home alright.

Bösendorfers' hire-fleet of pianos was expanding and there were more tune and attends. One such attendance, at the Royal Albert Hall, was for Marvin Hamlisch and the Boston Pops Orchestra. I was sitting in the room, behind the small doorway, which led straight out onto the concert platform. I had tuned the Imperial Concert Bösendorfer and asked Hamlisch if the piano was to his liking. He replied he was delighted. As the first half of the programme was underway, I was listening to the tuning of the orchestra, with the concert platform door closed; all the high frequencies of the instruments were blocked out, with all the middle and lower frequencies being conducted through the wooden structure of the concert platform. When listening to the brass section, especially the trombones, I could hear the tuning of the orchestra was not as good as it could be.

The sale of instruments to private customers was also on the increase. I had to follow up all of these pianos sales, check each piano out after delivery and give them a good tuning. There was the MP for Petersfield in Hampshire. On another occasion I caught the train to Coventry where I was to be met by the new client. I was told that I would instantly recognise him, for he had a pink Rolls Royce with white-wall tires. As we drove away from the station, I thought of Lady Penelope from Thunderbirds. Another new customer, who I was regularly visiting, to tune his newly purchased seven foot-four Bösendorfer, was Pete Townshend, the guitarist from The Who. Pete lived in a house in Twickenham overlooking the River Thames. There was a foot-bridge over to Eel Pie Island. Pete had his grand piano placed on the first floor. The staircase went up from the large sitting room, the walls of which were covered in hanging guitars. On one visit to Twickenham, Pete had a visitor; it was Andy "Thunderclap" Newman. I said "Hello" and ascended the stairs to do my tuning. Pete always brought me a cup of tea.

As well as all the work for Bösendorfers, I was building up quite a number of my own private clients. I was asked regularly, by passers-by, could I tune their piano. Also, the names of people needing pianos tuned were passed on to me from the ladies at the studio reception. The Wigmore studios stayed open until 8pm. The evening shift on reception was taken over by a Mister Brin. He had a uniform of grey clothe and a matching hat with black and red trim. His breast pocket was decorated with colour and medals he had received for his efforts in the Second World War. I would often stay and have a chat over a cup of tea, with Mr. Brin. I never knew his first name. He also passed on enquiries for piano tunings.

At the end of July 1972 it was my birthday. As there was no sign of getting a company car, I decided that I would buy my own. I looked in the columns of Exchange and Mart. I found myself looking at Rover cars for sale. As I read down the columns, I picked out a 1937 Rover Ten. The advert said that it was in Wembley. I rang the number and asked if the car was still for sale. The answer was "Yes", so I took the address and went off to view the vehicle. When I reached my destination the car was in the driveway. It was green. It had a long bonnet and a chrome radiator with large chrome headlights. I was looking inside at the green leather seats and the polished wooden dashboard; there was a voice that said "Do you like it?" The man took out a bunch of keys and unlocked the door and showed me under the bonnet, in the boot and then he said "Get in! I'll take you for a drive". On our return to his driveway I made him an offer of thirty-five pounds. He was asking for forty pounds. We shook hands at Thirty-seven pounds and fifty pence. The next evening I returned with the money and my insurance certificate, paid the man and drove away thrilled to bits with my new car. On the day of my birthday I received a hand made card. It was about twenty inches high and eight inches wide. It had been made by a Graphic Artist who worked nearby and she was a regular user of the Wigmore Studios. On the front of the card was a caricature of myself hanging, for dear life, from the glass chandelier in the piano showroom, and rising from the floor was a trio of black Bösendorfer concert grands, reaching up on their back legs, trying to tear me down. On the inside of the card it read "From all your friends at Wiggers Happy Birthday". As well as Bösendorfers, Habig Kimball the American parent company, had purchased another business called Herrburger Brookes. Their factory was just outside Nottingham. Michael and myself were to make a visit to Brookes. I was looking forward to this as I had never seen the manufacture of new piano parts, for Herrburger Brookes made piano actions and keys by their tens of thousands, for many different piano makers. On the day of our visit, Michael and myself took the train northwards. We were picked up at the station by the company manager. When we arrived at our destination, the factory manager showed us to his office. My eyes widened, for behind the bosses desk was a pair of enormous elephant tusks, placed directly behind his carved-back wooden chair. The tusks were secured on both sides of his chair to the floor. As they rose-up, the curved ends of the tusks crossed just before the pointed ends, even when the man stood up, the sculpture towered above his head. After refreshments and a chat it was time for our tour around the factory. The first room was the store full of various sizes of elephant tusks. The next room was where the tusks were graded and the process of making them into piano key covers. The ivory was cut with various saws and it was pointed out, the saw blades had no set on them. The set on any usual saw blade is when on the tooth of the saw bends out slightly and the next tooth of the saw blade bends the opposite way. This makes for a more efficient cut, but in doing so it sacrifices some of the material which ends up in saw dust. The ivory saw blade, with no set, was a slower process, but resulted in far less waste of the valuable ivory. The next shop was a much busier environment. There were a dozen men making the wooden piano keys. Lengths of wood were cut to the desired length and glued together. In the next process men were operating high speed band saws, cutting out the keys with the aid of a pattern guide for absolute accuracy. The next workshop was bigger and busier still, with dozens of women operating various machines, many driven by compressed air.

The workers manufactured, by the thousands, the various parts that make up the finished piano action.

Back at 38 Wigmore Street, as the end of the year approached, Michael and the American directors had a disagreement. Michael was not to return to his post in the New Year. As the New Year started I was in charge of all the tuning side of the business, so for the first time I had to keep a diary. As I now turn the pages of that old diary, the first month of the year 1973, I see entries were for tunings, for London Weekend Television, up to three tunings a day. Tuesday 2nd January, again I tuned for Pete Townshend at his house in Twickenham. There were tune and attend recording sessions at Smith's Square, with the singers Robert Tear and Benjamin Luxom. There were recording sessions at Kingsway Hall with Pavarotti, Emerson, Lake and Palmer at Advision Studios, The Faces, with Stevie Mariot at LWTV. February became even busier. Oscar Peterson on the Parkinson show. On the seventh of the month I did my first tuning for Top of The Pops and also Blue Peter. There were recording sessions at Decca Studios with Steven Pruslin and The Fires of London with Vanessa Redgrave doing some voice parts. Dudley Moore was performing at the Richmond Theatre and the most difficult job of my career, so far, was to tune the mighty Imperial Bösendorfer, directly below the whispering tower in St Paul's Cathedral.

By the end of February a new sales manager was appointed. Tony! He was a man in his late fifties and had been a piano salesman most of his life. He had moved from Manchester for his new appointment. I was starting to get dissatisfied with what I was earning. I was doing all the day-time tunings for my salary, but was receiving very little for my evening and weekend work. On discussing the matter with the new manager, Tony said that he would bring the matter to the attention of the American directors.

The last couple of weeks of March I spent at the newly built studios CTS, situated near Wembley Stadium. There was an orchestra made up of some forty musicians. Some of the musicians I had got to know from previous sessions. The singer was Harry Nilsson and the record, when finished, was called "A Little Touch of Schmilsson in the Night"(released June 1973). All this time I was still only earning just thirty pounds a week. It was during another discussion about the matter, with Tony, that the first seed of the idea of becoming free-lance passed through my mind. One day, while walking down the Edgware Road, I came across the piano shop called Jacques Samuels, The Bechstein Dealers. I decided to go in and look around. The showroom was extensive. As well as new and second hand Bechsteins, there were a dozen other makes. The salesman approached and asked if he could help. I told him I was a tuner and had just come in to look around. He enquired who I worked for. I told him Bösendorfers and previously Steinways. "You must be a good tuner. If you ever want a job we can always use another tuner". I told him I had been thinking of becoming freelance. He then said "If you ever do go self-employed, we can always provide you with as many tunings as you like". Over the next few weeks I contemplated the idea of working for myself. I had built up many private tunings, there was still work from Riva Gordon and now the offer of work from Jacques Samuels. I eventually brought up the subject with the manager of Bösendorfers. He said, of my idea, "It's always good for a young man to have a go and take his chances for himself in the world". He then said, "If I decided to go freelance then Bösendorfers would always use my services". There had been a recent sale of a Bösendorfer concert grand to one of the Rothschild's. I was to do the follow up tuning. The arrangements were made and when I arrived at the address in the New Forest I recognised the house, for I had been here before when I worked for Steinways. I rang the doorbell and presented myself. It was the same butler I remembered from my previous visit. I was shown through the house to where the newly installed instrument was. On my previous visit, while working for Steinways, there was a Steinway concert grand, married together with a Blüthner concert grand. Now the Steinway remained and the Blüthner was replaced by the Bösendorfer.

A few days later I had to tune and attend a concert at the Roundhouse. This was to be no ordinary recital. It was to be the world premiere of a new work by an Italian composer of whose name I have no recollection. I had been booked in at 4pm to tune the Imperial Bösendorfer, and upon my arrival there was an old battered Broadwood concert grand next to the instrument I was to tune. I also noticed a chaise-longue in the performance area. After tuning the Bösendorfer, I was playing a few chords when I was approached by the performer. He, in broken English, introduced himself. I asked him to try the piano. He sat at the keyboard and started to play. At first he played in a romantic style with lots of rolling arpeggios. Then he started to pound the piano in chords of violent discord, getting very excited in the process. He stopped playing and said the piano sounded wonderful. I then enquired the relevance of the Broadwood. He explained that part of his performance was to pull the strings and put pieces of metal on the strings and with two wooden mallets, to hit the inside of the old concert grand whilst holding down the sustain pedal. I thought to myself this one's a bit whacky. Continuing in his broken English he said that he would like to do this part of his composition on the Bösendorfer. I just stood there shaking my head saying, "If you do that you will have to pay for a new one". The Italian smiled and said this is why I have a pseudo piano. The performance was to start at 7.30pm and I was asked if I could be there at 7pm. After having found somewhere to eat I returned to the Roundhouse. I happened to notice many familiar faces from the music world gathering. I went and checked the Bösendorfer was alright. I noticed, next to the Broadwood, was, not only a pair of wooden hammers, but also a large heavy sledgehammer and three different colored buckets of water. As I retreated into the wings, the Italian composer approached me. He was holding what I thought was an old blanket. He then flung the garment around my shoulders. I quickly realised that it was not a blanket but a Monk's Habit. I said "What's this for?". He explained the first part of his performance was for me to walk on slowly up to the piano and make as if to tune it. I had little time to say no, so agreed to his request. At 7.30pm the house lights were dimmed and the platform was lit. With hood up and head stooped, I made my entrance. I walked over to the Bösendorfer, sat on the stool and with tuning lever in hand, I proceeded to make out I was tuning. I knocked out a couple of unisons and retuned them. Then my eyes nearly popped out. I had failed to notice, lying on the chaise longue, behind a transparent veil was a naked woman. I rose to my feet and left the stage as the audience applauded. The next part was the composer playing the Bösendorfer. The music was melodic and romantic. He gazed, as he played, with his eyes constantly on the naked woman. Then, as the piece progressed, the composer switched to the Broadwood, and without removing his gaze from the reclining beauty, proceeded with his pair of wooden hammers to hit the inside of the old instrument. This was followed by the buckets of water being thrown in. He then picked up the sledgehammer and started smashing the old Broadwood to bits. The violent, frenzied attack carried on for several minutes, when to the shock of everyone, a splinter of wood flew through the air like an arrow and pierced the naked woman's left breast. There was an instant gush of blood, a surprising end to a unique performance. A couple of weeks later I finally gave in my notice to Bösendorfers. I was now going to find my own way in the world.

GOING SOLO

Whilst serving my notice at Bösendorfers, I revisited Jacques Samuel's and had a chat with the manager, a Mr. Mandell. I told him I was about to start work for myself. He asked if I minded early morning tunings around the West End. I told him that I preferred that kind of work, rather than tramping round the suburbs doing private house tunings. So, by the middle of 1973 I was working solo, as well as regular visits to LWT TV and concert tunings for Bösendorfers. The work coming in from Jacques Samuels took me into many of the West End theatres. For example, every Monday morning was the pit piano at Drury lane. The show was "No, No Nanette" featuring a favourite song of mine, "Tea for Two". Also on Monday mornings was the Princess Theatre, for "Jesus Christ Superstar". There were more recording studios: Trident Studios, just off Wardour St, Soho; Landsdown Studios in Holland Park and Pie Studios at Marble Arch. There was a studio in Denmark St known as Tin Pan Alley, down in a basement was KPM studios, where they had a model A Steinway. This piano had been reconditioned by a small South London piano company, they had made quite a good job, but the tuning pins were not tight enough, so the tuning could not stay stable. On talking to the studio manager, cum recording engineer, I told him that the piano would never stay in tune with those loose pins. He asked me what could be done. I told him the piano would have to be repinned with larger size wrest pins. He asked me how long would it take and would the piano have to go into a workshop. I told him, I could do the job there, and it would take about two days, followed by several tunings over the next few days. He then asked "How much would it cost?" I told him that he would have to contact Jacques Samuels to get a price. He replied, "Can you do the job?" I replied "Yes". He then asked me "How much?" Knowing a set of wrest pins was about six pounds, I told him I could do the job for fifty-five pounds. He informed me that in a month's time the studio was closing for a week while a new recording desk was being fitted, could I do the job then. The arrangement was made.

I had made several visits to Landsdown Studios in Holland Park. The studio piano was a well worn Steinway model B. The studio manager was a man called Adrian Keridge and on most of my visits there he would be ranting and raving, shouting at all the studio staff. On one such a visit the tuning had to be done for 10am. I was running a bit late, the piano had taken a severe thrashing the session before. As I carried on with my tuning, I was surrounded by some thirty musicians warming up their instruments. Adrian Keridge was engineering the session. He was shouting instructions through the talk-back system, "First of all the drummer hit the bass drum only, then the snare drum". There were about six microphones around the kit. I was struggling to tune up the treble and constantly watching the clock. After the turn of the drums, it was the brass players, followed by the string section. By the time Adrian had gone around the rest of the instruments, I had managed to finish my tuning at three minutes past ten. On the way up the stairs, coming out of the studio, I passed the control room door. Out came Adrian shouting and bellowing at me for "Holding up the session!". I told him I was sorry but the piano was in an awful state and I had only gone over three minutes. By now Adrian was red in the face from going on, so I told him to, "Sod off!" and left the building. On occasion, some mornings could be quite a dash around of up to a dozen tunings to be done before ten in the morning, after which I would buy a paper and have breakfast. Around mid-morning I would fit in a visit to a private house. On one such a job, was in St John's Wood and on the tuning card from Jacques Samuels was the name Paul McCartney. The address took me to a large house in a quiet road, not far from Abbey Road Studios. The housekeeper answered the door. I entered and was shown to the room to where the piano was situated. As we passed the kitchen I peered through the door. I remember lots of wood and gingham curtains and table cloth. The door in front of me was opened. I entered a large room with high ceilings. I raised the lid of the Bechstein grand. The housekeeper asked if I would like a cup of tea and left the room. I started my tuning, my tea was delivered and I was left alone. Other than the grand piano, there were two enormous JBL speakers and several shelves with hundreds of records, the rest of the room was covered with various sized cushions. Another mid-morning tuning was to a large detached house situated between Holland Park and Kensington High St. The house of red brick had circular towers with round red pointed roofs. The owner of the house was Richard Harris, the actor, songwriter and director. On entering, I was again greeted by the housekeeper. The interior was like a medieval castle and what I remember the most is that all the electrical switches were in small, almost invisible cupboards, which were set into the wall. This, I suppose was not to spoil the effects of the décor.

By now it was time to start the re-pinning of KPM's Steinway. After my morning dash around the studios and theatres I arrived in Tin-Pan Ally. I first of all removed the piano action and keys and placed the mechanism underneath the piano for safe keeping; with the aid of one of the engineers we removed the heavy piano lid. The first job was to remove one of the wrest pins. Then I legged it to Covent Garden where Fletcher and Newman, the piano parts company, was. The small trade counter was just off the street. As a part of my toolkit I had not yet got myself a wrest pin gauge, a piece of metal, with several holes of different sizes, each one representing the different sizes of wrest pins available. I asked the man behind the counter if I could have a set of wrest pins a whole size bigger. He took his wrest pin gauge out of his pocket, pushed through my pattern and said "You need a three O". O was the means of measuring wrest pins. I had made many visits to Fletcher and Newman's and was getting familiar with the counter staff. While the man was getting my set of wrest pins, there was a short friendly Irishman, there his job was cutting felts and leathers. He pushed a small package into my hand, he said "Put it up under your arm, inside your jacket". I did as I was told. The man returned with my box of wrest pins. I paid and left. I returned to Denmark Street. I opened the parcel I was given. It was lots of off-cuts of felts and leathers. This was not to be the last time the little Irishman passed me a parcel of off-cuts of felts and leathers. Around half-past eleven I started the job in hand. Replacing wrest pins, in any make of piano, is probably one of the worst of all jobs. First of all each wrest pin would be turned anti-clockwise one whole turn. This task was done using a T hammer. After ten to fifteen minutes, every string had been slackened. The next operation was to use a small screwdriver and prise out of the small hole the high tensile music wire, which coiled around the pin. Next was to turn out the wrest pin from the pin block. Approximately a dozen turns would release the pin. Then a new over-sized wrest pin was rubbed with chalk into the fine threads. Chalking the pins would help give the tuning pin a smooth feel. Then I pushed the pin through the coil of wire, pushing the end of the wire through a small hole located in the side of the wrest pin. Next with the aid of a pin punch, the pin was hammered into the pin block. Then another tool, called a coil lifter, was placed around the coil of wire, wrapped around the wrest pin and levered upwards at the same time as tightening the string. This job was to be repeated another two hundred and forty times. Throughout this process, often the sharp end of the wire would spring and could sink itself into the end of a finger or thumb. By the time I had finished the job around 5pm the next day, my hands were covered in small punctures and scratches. The next job was to put the strain on the instrument. This was done by means of pulling every string on the piano up to concert pitch in approximately twenty minutes. Then I returned the action and keys from underneath the piano and replaced it in the instrument. I checked the mechanism. The sound engineer shouted, "That sounds awful". I replied "It will be fine after half a dozen tunings". The re-pin had been a success, as now, the wrest pins were firm and tight and also smooth to the feel. Throughout the two days hard work the studio tape operator had looked after me with cups of tea and he had been taking an interest in what I had done. I then asked him, that in any spare time he might have, if he could strike each note severely hard several times, as this would help the settling down of the strings. I then packed up my tools and told him that I would call in the next day and give the piano another tuning. After the usual rush around the early tunings, I returned to Tin Pan Alley for a repeat tuning of the Steinway. The tape operator had certainly given the instrument a sever pounding as the tuning was almost non-existent. He told me he had pounded through each note at least a dozen times. I repeated the process every day, including Saturday, by which time the piano was staying in tune. The following Monday the studio was re-opened, with its new sixteen track recording facility and its re-pinned piano.

Another new tuning job I had secured was for the Covent Garden Dance Centre. Three pianos to be tuned once a month. On one such a visit I was tuning the upright piano in the largest dance studio. The walls were covered in mirrors and the ceiling rose up like the roof of a church. High up, perched on a window was one of the parrots. There were two parrots that were kept in cages. When the studios were not being used the birds were set free to stretch their wings. As I started my tuning, the parrot swooped down, above my head and out of nowhere, landed on my head, sinking his claws through my thick curly hair, which was now quite long. I shot to my feet waving my arms, the parrot finally let go and returned to his roost. I kept my eyes firmly fixed on that parrot. I finished my tuning and was using both hands to replace the fall and top door into piano, when here he came again, trying to perch on my head. I ran to the door clutching my tuning bag. On further visits I always went through the door of the studio holding my tuning lever by the short end, waving it around like a football rattle, keeping an eye open for my feathered friend.

One Sunday I was spending the day with my girlfriend of several months. I had just one tuning that day. The piano had been supplied by Jacques Samuels and delivered to Hammersmith Odeon. The artist was Fats Domino. We arrived backstage just before midday. Other than the doorman, the place was deserted. The piano was in the middle of the stage. My girlfriend walked around the stage as I started my tuning. Out of the wings came this lone figure. He came over and said Hello. He was a very well dressed Black American with a sharp suit, bright red waist coat, patent leather shiny shoes and his attire was finished of with lots of gold rings, watches and bracelets and even a gold tooth. He told us he was the guitarist for the band. He then engaged my girlfriend in conversation. I heard him ask her if he could show her around the theatre. A few minutes later she came back screaming through the wings. I said "What's wrong?" She replied "That man got me into his dressing room and dropped his trousers!" I laughed and said, "That will teach you for wandering off with strangers".

Starting in September 1973, I was making visits to Sarm Studios in Brick Lane. Sarm boasted the first twenty-four track recording studio in England. The piano was taking a severe pounding from the composer Robert John Godfrey. On one late afternoon visit to Sarm, Robert asked if I could stay for the evening session, as it was going to be solo piano and he wanted the piano kept in trim. He told me he would pay me direct and we agreed terms of twenty-five pounds until midnight. As Robert finished a take he would go into the control room to listen back. While he was doing this I would go into the studio and tweak any notes that had gone out of tune. The session finished at 1am. Robert thanked me and handed me 5, five pound notes, then an extra fiver, as we went an hour over our agreed time. As I drove home, through a deserted city of London, I was chuckling to myself as I had earned more in one evening than an average man could earn in a week. Coming up to Christmas I was tuning at the BBC TV Centre. In the same studio was a man assembling a drum kit. He came and introduced himself. "My name is Maurice". He told me that he had a musical instrument hire company. Then he asked me who I worked for. I told him that I was freelance. Then he pulled out his card and handed it to me and asked if I could come and see him in the New Year. The second week of January, I visited Maurice in his warehouse, which was situated in Jedo Road, Shepherd's Bush. Maurice greeted me and immediately gave me a tour of the ground floor. There were racks of guitars and amplifiers. There was a percussion department, with assorted drum kits, timpanis and gongs. Further down the warehouse, stacked high, were mountains of PA equipment. Another department was purely for keyboards. I was familiar with some of the instruments as I had seen them in various studios. There were Fender Rhodes, Wurlitzer electric pianos, Hohner clavinets and Hammond organs. Adjacent to this area were a couple of rooms with electronic engineers working on amplifiers, guitars and keyboards. I followed Maurice upstairs to his office. Maurice's wife was working at a desk doing paperwork and answering the constantly ringing telephone. Maurice sat down at his desk and I sat down opposite and he asked me how I had got into pianos. I told him my history so far. Then he told me he wanted to expand his keyboard department as he was regularly being asked for acoustic pianos. He then asked if I wanted a job. I told him I had some regular tunings of my own and also wanted to expand my new business. Maurice then asked me if I could come and see him later in the week.

Although, by now, I had tunings coming in from Bösendorfers, Jacques Samuels and an embryonic group of my own customers, even so, there were some days with no work at all. I revisited Jedo Road mid-morning the following Friday. I was greeted by Maurice. He immediately asked if I wanted a job. I replied "Not full time". "I thought you would say that" replied Maurice. He then said, "If you give me a couple of days a week in the workshop, and also give me first refusal on your time, I'll give you fifty pounds a week retainer and a company vehicle". This all came as a bit of a surprise. He then informed me that he had bought a Steinway grand piano from a studio in Chalk Farm and it was arriving the following week. The following Monday I had finished any tunings I had and made my way to Jedo Road. Maurice had a small area in the keyboard storeroom all ready for my arrival. There were two modern upright pianos, a little on the worn side. I set about honing these instruments. While I did this, the sound of electric guitars, drums and the constant banter and yodeling of the hirsute members of staff. There was a bang on the door. "Want a cup of tea mate? My name's Robert". We shook hands and he handed me a mug of tea. Robert was like nobody I had worked alongside with before. Instead of what I was used to – collars, ties and suits. Robert was denim clad, with hair down to his waist. My own hair was only over my ears.

As I got to know my new hirsute work mates, I discovered some were roadies between jobs, like Pat, who was tall with long red hair. He was known as "Mono" as he had lost his hearing in one ear. He had just returned from a tour with Hot Chocolate. Other people were musicians between gigs. This posse of hairy workers used a small fleet of transit vans and were constantly in and out, delivering equipment all around London. As I worked on the two upright pianos, I was visited periodically by different members of staff who were interested in what I was up to. Everyone was there because of their interest in music and everyone was most interested in the workings of a piano and even more fascinated when I started tuning. As well as the two uprights, there was a double manual harpsichord and a Baldwin electric harpsichord. These instruments I checked and tuned the following week.

One of the new jobs from Bösendorfers, was for another model seven foot four, which had been purchased by Pete Townshend for The Who's new studio, Ramport. Unlike most other recording studios, which were in and around the West End, Ramport was situated in the middle of a council estate in Wandsworth. When I first tuned the new Bösendorfer in its purpose built soundproof booth, I noticed, unlike all other studios I had visited, where, in the control rooms would be two large loud speakers, at Ramport, there were four. Quadraphonic had arrived.

The next time I went to Jedo Road, Maurice had bought a new upright piano. This was a Broadwood, with a jangle strip fitted. This was a piece of wood which was connected to each end of the piano by a hinge. Attached to this strip of wood were eighty-eight strips of thin leather, approximately two inches long. At the end of each strip was a brass rivet pierced into the leather. When the strip was lowered, it was done by pulling a lever under the keyboard. The strips would come in line with the strings and as the hammers were struck the rivet would hit the string. This made the piano sound very metallic and jangly. The sound of the jangle piano would be recognised in the theme music for the television soap, EastEnders.

The electronic engineers were in the next workshop keeping all the gear in full working order, including the amplifiers, which were mostly valve: Marshal, Fender, Orange and the Solid State H&H. Another one of the jobs the engineers had to do was to keep the Fender Rhodes, the Wurlitzer electric pianos, Clavinets and Hammond organs, all working, and to keep them in tune. I was looking inside a Fender Rhodes stage piano as one of the engineers was tuning it. Instead of using his ears he was tuning it with the aid of an electronic tuning device. He had been working on the keyboard for over two hours and had still not finished. He was moaning that he had two more to tune. I started to examine how the Fender Rhodes functioned. The principal was very much like an ordinary piano. There was the key and when depressed this pushed a hammer upwards, the action was in no way as sophisticated as a modern grand piano. There was just a plastic cam which pushed up a hammer made of plastic, with a rubber tip glued to the end. The hammers hit a tyne, this was a length of round steel, varying in length, from around an inch long in the extreme treble graduating down to several inches long in the extreme bass. The tyne, although varying in length, were all of the same thickness, slightly thinner than a match. On each length of tyne was a small spring. This was the way the instrument was tuned. I watched the engineer push, with a small screwdriver, the spring along the tyne. This, in effect, was a simple, tunable tuning fork. The sound was picked up by a small pick-up, one for each note. I asked the engineer if I could have a go on the next tuning. "With pleasure" he replied. The next Rhodes was set up in my workshop. I set about the tuning in the same way as a normal piano. I struck my middle C tuning fork and placed it between my teeth. Pressing middle C on the keyboard, it was slightly flat. I pushed with my small screwdriver the spring, it was much tighter than I expected. After a little trial and error I got the hang of it. As I progressed, setting the chromatic scale, I gained speed, compared with the tuning of a traditional piano, it was so easy. There were no unisons to tune and once the note was in tune it stayed there, not like having to set in tune the two hundred and twenty strings on a conventional piano. I finished the last note of the Rhodes in about forty minutes. I went through to the electronic workshop and told them that I had finished. The engineers were a bit surprised at the little time it had taken me. Then one engineer asked "Do you mind if we check it on our machine?" All the engineers gathered round as the machine was plugged in.

The small screen on the device had a line down the middle. If when the corresponding note was struck, it flickered to the right if the note was sharp, and if the note flickered to the left, the note was flat. When it flickered down the center the note was in tune. As the engineer worked his way through the whole compass, the machine flickered down the center of every note. "Bet you can't do that with a Clavinet?" said one of the Boffins. "Well, drag one in and I'll have a go!" I replied. In no time at all the Hohner clavinet was set up. I asked to be shown the principle of how it worked. First of all, removing two screws, a metal cover, the whole length of the keyboard came away revealing a line of slotted screws, one for each note. I looked under the keys and I could see how the instrument worked. It was based on a Clavichord, a keyboard instrument dating back some three hundred years. There was a single string for each note on the ancient Clavichord, there was a small brass tangent which came into contact with the string when the key was depressed. On the Clavinet the string was trapped by a rubber pad onto a raised metal bed. When the note was played the tuning of the Clavinet was adjusted by the slotted screws, which on further examination turned out to be the same as a guitar machine head. The Boffins then left me to it. Each slotted machine head was marked which note it corresponded to. I quite soon realised why I had been taunted by the challenge of tuning one of these keyboards. With it being a stringed instrument, it was very unstable. Not only that the way the string was trapped by the rubber pad, one could slightly sharpen the note by pressing harder. I soon realised that tuning the Clavinet was just the same as tuning the piano, one had to set the strings in tune by giving the note a severe strike thus settling the string. The Clav or Clavi as the Clavinet was more commonly known was the Funk instrument of the Seventies and the most famous opening riff the Clavi was used for was Stevie Wonder's 'Superstition'.

The next electric keyboard I learnt to tune and maintain was the Wurlitzer electric piano. This keyboard had a roller escapement action, in miniature, just like a modern grand piano action. The small felt hammers hit a single reed. At the end of the reed was a small blob of solder. Removing a small amount of the solder of the end of the reed would sharpen the note; adding a small amount of solder would flatten it. Tuning the Wurlitzer could be a hazardous business, as the way the pick-up worked was by the reed vibrating between a slot in a metal strip. When viewed in the hole, it looked like a large metal cone. The danger came from several hundred volts DC being passed through the metal strip, so one had to switch off the power every time to make an adjustment. The Wurlitzer became a part of the distinct sound of the band SuperTramp.

ONWARDS AND UPWARDS

O ver the few months of being self-employed my income increased dramatically, and added together with my retainer from Maurice, it was time to move out of bedsit land. A suitable house was found in the suburb of Heston. The house was of modern design with two double bedrooms, luxury bathroom, open-plan sitting room, incorporating a large modern kitchen and gas central heating. I was to share this with my friend John, who was a self-employed carpenter. It was handy for the move, as Maurice had now supplied me with a vehicle, a new mini van with Maurice's logo written on the sides. My pre-war trusty Rover, which had served me well, was now surplus to requirements. I parked it up in Jedo Road with a for sale notice in the windscreen. It sold quite quickly for seventy-five pounds, double what I paid for it.

The next piano to arrive was the Steinway Maurice had bought from the studio in Chalk Farm. "What do you think of it?" asked Maurice. On inspection of the little grand piano, a 1930's Model M, I told him, "Not a lot so far". The casework was ebonized black. Although not too battered, it was covered in filth. I pulled out the action - what a mess. The strings were corroded, covered in red rust and the bass strings had lost all of their tone. The action was totally worn out. The hammers, in the treble, had worn through the felt, right through to the wood. I used my dusting brush to reveal the bridges and check the sound-board. Maurice was keen to know what had to be done. I told him everything. "Can you do it?" asked Maurice. I said "Yes". Then Maurice said "Well get on with it. Just ask for anything you need". I completely reconditioned the little Steinway. With all my other commitments it took me a couple of months before the instrument was ready for hire. Added to the stock of keyboards for hire, Maurice had bought one single manual harp-sichord and a large double manual harpsichord. So, I was now tuning traditional pianos, harpsichords, Fender Rhodes, Wur-litzer's and of course the Clavinet. I was discovering more and more studios where these instruments were being constantly used. Many of these venues were around the West End – Ad-vision Studios, Command Studios and Pie Studios. On my visits to Pie Studios I would descend down the stairs and I would be greeted by the smell of disinfectant from the freshly mopped corridor floors. There were also out of town studios such as the Manor, near Oxford. This studio was an old manor house, with its own grounds and was owned by Richard Branson. There was accommodation in the rustic old house, so bands could stay for the duration of their recordings. Two enormous Irish wolf-hounds seemed permanently sprawled over the flagstones of the kitchen floor. On many visits to the Manor Studios, Richard Branson could always be seen in the same woolly jumper, both elbows worn out and threadbare.

Around the spring of 1974, Ramport was becoming busy. I was tuning the Bösendorfer regularly, for The Who were busy mak-ing the soundtrack for the film 'Tommy'. On Sunday 12th May, I was to tune and attend for the session. It was Elton John recording 'Pin Ball Wizard'. The following Saturday, May 18 was my first outdoor football stadium concert. I had to be at Charl-ton Athletic Football Ground no later than 10.30am. Packed in the little Mini van was a Fender stage piano, Wurlitzer and Clavinet. I had the aid of Pat the roadie, who was to help me unload the keyboards. As we drove through South-East London we stopped at a greasy spoon for a fry-up. Pat and myself were not feeling too good as we didn't crawl out of the Speakeasy until the small hours. On arrival at Charlton, we unloaded the gear and humped it on stage. We were greeted by Lindisfarne's roadies. One of them said "Here's your breakfast boys", handing Pat and myself a bottle of Newcastle Brown Ale. As I was going through the tuning of the keyboards, the crowd had started gathering. It was a brilliant, cloudless sunny day and the sea of thousands of faces in the crowd turned from pale to red by the end of the afternoon. An enormous roar came from the crowd as Lindisfarne opened the show. I was tuning that day for Maggie Bell followed by Lou Reed. As I was on and off stage I can remember the vast PA system. On the backs of the various speaker cabinets were the logos for The Who, Led Zeppelin and Elton John. All these speakers had been joined together to make one almighty wall of sound. The Who started their set just as it was getting dark. The crowd went wild as the first chords for the song "Substitute" rang out.

The next week I made my first visit to Shepperton Studios. I had keyboards to tune for the band Uriah Heap. The following Sunday was a very different stadium concert. It was the first hire of the little Steinway grand. There was a Fender Rhodes to tune for the warm-up band Showaddywaddy. The crowd for the event was probably the nearest thing to Beatle mania. Thousands of out of control teenage girls screaming for the start of the show for David Cassidy at White City Football Ground. After watching Showaddywaddy going through their polished routine, it was time to check the Steinway. As I sat at the piano, even with a loud monitor, it was hard to hear what I was doing, as the frenzied crowd was getting out of control. Young girls were being lifted by the security men over the metal fence barrier as the crush to get nearer to the front became more frantic. As I was tuning there were pleas for the crowd to settle down. Eventually David Cassidy and his troupe started his act. As the show progressed the news went round backstage that one of the young girls had died in the crush. Even after the show, as we wheeled the Steinway off the stage, dozens of screaming girls, tried stretching their arms through the security fence, hoping to touch the little grand piano their hero had played. The next of these outdoor concerts I was to tune various keyboards for, fell on my birthday July 27th.

The venue was in the grounds of Crystal Palace and was known as the Crystal Palace Garden Party. The landscape made a natural amphitheatre. At the bottom of the slopes there was a small lake and on the other side of the water was the stage covered with a circular dome. I spent the day tuning for Leo Sayer, Procol Harum and headlining was Rick Wakeman.

At White City tuning for David Cassidy

One evening the telephone rang, it was Adrian Kerridge from Landsdown studios. He told me he had done a session at KPM studios and was very impressed by the sound of the Steinway. I said to Adrian, "Do you remember who I am? I told you to sod off once". He replied, "I don't care about that. I just want my Steinway to sound as good as the one at KPM", so another studio piano tuning was added to my list. Next came the odd tuning from the Beatles' studio Apple. This studio was famous for the time the Beatles played on the roof. The front of the building, for years, was covered in scaffolding. At the back of the Marquee Club, in Wardour Street Soho, was a small studio. I made several visits there tuning for Linsey de Paul. Come September I had been booked by Maurice for the whole day and evening. The little black Steinway had been booked by Mel Bush the promoter. This was for an all-American line up. All the gear had been flown in from the States for the one-off concert. Just a grand piano and a tuner were needed. The venue was my first gig at Wembley Stadium, and the line up was The Band, Joni Mitchell backed by Tom Scott and the LA Express followed by Crosby, Stills, Nash and Young. Each of these performers were going to use the little grand piano and it was to be tuned before every performance. The little black Steinway was delivered onto the stage by 10am. Everywhere were the American road crew setting up the back line. As I started tuning, I watched as the microphones were being positioned. As things got louder and louder, I found it hard to hear what I was tuning, so I had to ask for a monitor. As the Steinway had been fitted with a piano pick-up, it was soon plugged into the nearest stage box. A wedge monitor was placed by my side and a little later I could hear the piano through the speaker. This was also an opportunity for the sound engineer to check the sound of the piano, for while I was tuning at many thousand of watts, the little Steinway sounded enormous. As I struck a note the PA system delivered the tones, reverberating around the stadium. At twelve noon the first band to perform was Jesse Colin Young. There was the most enormous roar from the crowd. I listened to the piano. The hammers on the little grand, I had pulled over with sandpaper revealing the hard felt below the surface which gave the instrument an almost metallic sound. It was necessary to do this so the sound of the piano would cut through the mix. The little black grand was repositioned on the stage. I had been asked by 'The Band's' road crew if I would check the tuning. This time the stadium was full of people, over seventy thousand of them. Adjacent to the little Steinway had been set up the most enormous multi-manual electric organ. When "The Band" started, thousands of people cheered. By the end of the first song the whole of the crowd on the football pitch were in a haze of marijuana smoke. After the bands dynamic performance, it was time to check and tune the little black piano for Joni Mitchell. She arrived on stage wearing a fur coat. I thought "it's not cold". Listening to the harmonies and the quality of Joni Mitchell's voice was my first experience of American harmony singing in a live show. For this set, the piano had been moved towards the centre of the stage and as she played the little black Steinway. I peered through the back line and thought the piano looks tiny on that enormous stage. I was completely amazed at the performance given by Joni Mitchell. After she had finished the Steinway was moved into position, next to a Hammond B3. As I finished tuning, I checked the piano was in unison with the Hammond. Next a man wearing a gangster style hat asked me if the keys were in tune? I told him "Everything was sounding good". I didn't realise until the band got ready to start their set that the man wearing the hat was Neil Young. This came to light when one of the bands shouted "Where did you get that hat Neil?" Neil Young's two Fender amplifiers had been meticulously placed on stage. In front of the two Fender amplifiers was placed a woven carpet. In the centre of the two amps was the skull of a beast with its two horns intact and leaning against the other amplifier was his favourite set of golf clubs. The sun was starting to set as Crosby, Stills, Nash and Young started to play. Later in their set Joni Mitchell joined in making more heavenly harmonies. This was a truly wonderful day.

The next week it was back to early studio tunings. Landsdown, by now, kept me the busiest. Monday usually started with a production team who had flown in from Paris. The studio had been booked for the whole day, with a line up of some forty musicians. At 10am it was 'Take One'. Other than the odd tea break, these sessions could go on until the late evening, after which, the production team flew home to Paris, with their music in the can. A regular user of Landsdown was Dave Clark, producing various line-ups. On the occasions Johnny Pearson was recording, I would often have to tune and attend for these sessions as the piano was the lead instrument. Johnny Pearson made many theme tunes for television programmes. I remember distinctly the day the music for 'All Creatures Great and Small' was recorded. Mike Batt often booked two or three days at a time, and the piano was booked to be tuned for each session. The songs Mike Batt was writing and recording were for the 'Wombles'. A new studio I had gained for regular tuning was Mayfair Sound. The studio was on the first and second floors of the building next door to the Post Office in South Molton Street, Mayfair.

One Sunday I had a call from the road manager of the band Soft Machine. They were in need of a grand piano for their gig at the Rainbow. He told me he had forgotten to book a piano and was in deep trouble. I took his telephone number and told him that I would call him back within the hour. I went to a lot of trouble to get a piano together and a van, and the help I needed to deliver the instrument. The show went on. I was given a cheque from the road manager. Two weeks later the cheque bounced for the third and final time.

The little black Steinway, of Maurice's, was regularly hired out. On one occasion I was booked to tune it for Procol Harum. The venue was the nineteen thirties ballroom above Bebbas in Kensington High Street. I was tuning the little black Steinway when Gary Booker arrived. Instead of looking like a rock star, he looked more like a city gent - pinstriped suit, black overcoat and finished off with a bowler hat.

The latter months of 1974 became even more busy, right up until New Years Eve. There were the early studio tunings, followed by a full day at the BBC TV Centre. I had tuned the piano for Play School in studio five. Then I went to studio six to tune two grand pianos for the Old Grey Whistle Test New Year's Eve Special, featuring the band Ace, performing their hit 'How Long'. There was Tom Jones and his band, and the loudest was the band Bad Company. Eventually they failed to perform as they refused to turn down their instruments and the excessive volume was interfering with the television cameras. There was not even a day off on New Year's Day, with several studio tunings and back to the Television Centre for the live broadcast of the New Year's Day Top of The Pops. The piano was for the Johnny Pearson Orchestra, for many of the performers would sing live to the orchestra's backing. The day finished off at the BBC TV Theatre for a New Year's Day show featuring Lulu. Occasionally I would tune various keyboards for a studio over the river in Barnes. The complex was Olympic. There were many keyboards tuned there used by the Rolling Stones.

At the old De Lane Lea studios in Soho, one mid-morning, I wondered what was wrong with the Steinway. There were muffled notes, buzzing notes and an unpleasant smell. I raised the lid of the model B and the whole of the instrument was covered in fish and chip wrappings, with a few odd chips sitting on the strings. I removed the grease ridden wrappings and tuned the piano. On my way out I asked the studio receptionist "What dirty sods were in the studio last?" she replied "The Bee Gees".

One Saturday morning I had a call from Maurice. He told me there had been a request for an upright piano. The piano was on the van and the boys were on their way to Hampstead. Maurice gave me the address and asked if I could be there as soon as possible. When I arrived it turned out to be a flat I had visited before. This was the home of the singer and keyboard player Ann Odell. The humpers had just finished delivering the piano. I removed the panels from the upright and started my tuning. There was a very attractive woman making snacks for a couple of children. Then a voice behind me said "Hello, don't bother with the black notes. I can only play in C". I cracked up laughing, turned round to be greeted with a handshake, it was Ringo. I finished my tuning for Ringo, including the black notes.

ACQUIRING MY FIRST STEINWAY GRAND

I had recently tuned an old model A Steinway grand for a client in Highgate. He told me he wanted the piano to be sounding good as he was going to sell it. I asked him how much he wanted for the instrument. He replied, "Three-hundred and fifty pounds". I told him that I would let him know if I came across anybody that was looking for such a piano. The ancient model A retained its tone but was in need of full renovation. Dashing around tuning all the time, always on the move, almost panicking so as not to be late for any sessions, I missed working in one place with my apron on at the bench. The model A Steinway kept going through my mind. I almost had enough money to buy the instrument, but where would I put it. I tuned a Bösendorfer which was being delivered by Fred from Piano Transport. I told Fred that I was thinking of buying a Steinway grand but had no where to put it. Fred told me to go and see Challens in Camden Town. The next time I was in Camden, I went and sought out Challens workshop. I found the premises in a narrow backstreet of old Victorian warehouses and workshops. I knocked on the door. I heard a voice, "Come in". I was greeted by the familiar smell of French polish and the glue pot. There were three men and a women drinking tea. All of them were knocking on a bit. "Can I help you?" said one of the men. I told him Fred, from Piano Transport, suggested that I come and see you. I told the man I was a tuner and I was looking for a small space to work on a Steinway grand. "That's a bit posh" said one of the other men. I was given a mug of tea, just like the pint mugs I remember from Wilson and Pecks. At the end of the meeting I was offered a corner of the workshop and a bench to work on for three pounds a week. Having left Challens workshop, I immediately found a phone box and called to see if the Steinway was still for sale. He replied "Yes". I offered him Three Hundred pounds. He then asked "How will you pay?" I told him that I would pay him in cash. "Done", was his reply. I rang Piano Transport and arranged collection of the instrument. On the day of the shift I arrived at my clients and paid him the money. Fred arrived with his crew and an hour later the piano was on its legs in Challens workshop. I paid a months rent in advance, put on my apron and set about pulling the old model A apart.

It was familiar ground working at Challens, for the few skilled men making the last of the Challen pianos had all worked in the piano industry all of their life. One such a character was Jimmy, the French polisher, or more commonly known in the trade as 'a shiner'. Jimmy, a man well past retirement age told me of the different piano manufacturers he had worked for. He then added that there were over a hundred different piano makers around the North London area when he was an apprentice in the 1920's. By early 1975 work came streaming in, more and more I was being contacted by clients directly. Throughout the different recording studios and different venues there was a communication network between all of the receptionists. Wherever I was working, I would let the girls on reception know where I was going for my next call. On occasion, when I could not be found, within a few calls I could be sifted out, for the music industry at this period was an intimate community. I now had two new studios on my list. Scorpio Sound, a new Yamaha grand to be tuned once a week or more if requested. The other new client was for George Martin Studios, Air. Air studios were located on the top floor of a building on the corner of Oxford Circus. George Martin had recently bought two new Bösendorfers. A concert grand for studio one and a seven-foot four for studio two. As well as the new grands, there was the, in house Rhodes, Clavi, Wurlitzer and the Baldwin electric harpsichord. I was gaining a reputation, as I had never advertised nor did I even have a business card. I now told Maurice that I did not want his retainer any more as I could not spare the two days a week. Maurice was upset at my decision. I assured Maurice that I would still do any tunings. I handed Maurice the keys to the mini van and went straight off to buy a car of my own.

By now, my friend Pat, the roadie, was working for the Rubett's, constantly touring the country. Whenever he was in London, Pat would track me down, to tune the band's Fender Rhodes and Clavinet. He once tracked me down to a wine bar in the Kings Road. This watering hole was a favourite of many of my new musical mates. The girl behind the bar shouted, "Terry, Pat's on the phone" On answering, Pat said, he was on his way. When Pat came in the door, he told me he had parked the truck nearby. I asked him "How can I tune without an amplifier?" Pat opened the back of the seven ton lorry. It was piled high with the PA back line and drum kit. Pat had put the keyboards on last, so we could get to them. I still had no answer to my question, when Pat pulled out of a box a tiny little amplifier. "Look at this" said Pat "Battery powered!" This new little amplifier was called 'A PigNose 7-100'. As I tuned the two keyboards, on the back of the lorry parked in the Kings Road, there were many strange looks from the people passing by.

I had spent every spare hour working on my Steinway and had managed to finish it by late spring. Having mentioned to Maurice that I was restoring another Steinway, he immediately expressed interest. I sold my model A to Maurice for one thousand four hundred and fifty pounds. The model A was soon put to work. The first band to hire it was the band Yes, on Saturday

10th of May, an all day event at Queen's Park Rangers Football Ground. I was booked to tune and be in attendance. The next time I was booked to look after the model A was for the Osmond's at Earls Court. I knew the Osmond's were in town, for I had tuned a grand piano in a studio opposite Broadcasting House. This was not a recording session but more of a PR for the Osmond's. As I tuned the grand, all of the Osmond's came in. They congregated around the piano, just as a herd of photographers and journalists poured in. Immediately all of the Osmond's switched on a huge smile. I thought they looked like an advert for McLean's. On Sunday 1st of June I was attending to the model A, along with other keyboards. I had done the ground work on these various instruments the previous day, for the first performance of Rick Wakeman's, 'The Myths and Legends of King Arthur and the Knights of the Round Table'. The whole of the floor area of the Empire Pool had been made into an ice rink. I decided to stay and watch the extravaganza and enjoyed very much the music, the songs and the ice dancers. The next time with the model A, along with me to tune, was the summer garden party at Crystal Palace. Among the performers were Steeleye Span, John Cale, Jack Bruce but most of all I remember Steve Harley and Cockney Rebel. There had been installed a platform, just below the surface of the water, at the front of the stage and at one point, Steve Harley stepped out onto the hidden platform, as if to appear that he was walking on water.

On Friday the 4th of July, I went in the truck, with the boys from Maurice Placquet. There was the model A on board, along with Fender Rhodes, Clavinet, Hammond B3 and various back line amplifiers. The stage at Knebworth was enormous and over twenty feet high. When it was time to unload the Steinway, the only way of getting it on the stage was to use a lift, which was a most precarious contraption, being like a fork-lift truck, two metal prongs were attached to the scaffolding, which the stage was made of. The piano was placed on the two metal prongs.

Someone had to stand on the Heath Robinson device, pull a lever and the lift would rise. It was a unanimous decision, that person would be me. On the first attempt, I panicked and let go of the lever. Luckily I had only gone up a couple of feet when I let go of the handle and the piano and I dropped to the ground with a thump. Someone yelled "Don't let go of the handle until you reach the top". The next attempt was successful and the piano was safely on the stage. Having put the Steinway on its legs and checked the instrument, I then checked the Fender Rhodes and Clavinet, and then all the instruments were covered in a tarpaulin. There was no point in tuning any of the keyboards as they needed to acclimatise. I returned the next day and was on stage by 8am. It was coming up to eleven o'clock when I was satisfied all of the instruments were in tune. The stage manager told me he wanted me to stay backstage so I could check the keyboards, as necessary, throughout the day. I enjoyed listening to Roy Harper, Captain Beefheart and a favourite of mine Linda Lewis. I popped on stage throughout the day to check the instruments. While doing the final preparations for Pink Floyd, Graham Chapman did some sketches from Monty Python. It was early evening and the sun was going down. The stage was set. I left the back stage area, tuning bag in hand. I had decided to make my way to my car. I left the stage area and slowly made my way through the crowd. I kept close to the perimeter fence. Halfway up the slope I turned round to look back at the stage and sat down to have a smoke. There was an eerie quiet from the biggest crowd I had ever seen. Just as the sun was about to set, I could hear a roaring noise. First of all I thought that there was something wrong with the PA system. Then as quick as lightening, two World War Two spitfires came flying out of the setting sun and flew directly over the stage. The two planes were flying so low I could see the pilots waving. The two spitfires had gone as quickly as they had arrived. The applause from the crowd was deafening. Pink Floyd opened their set with 'Echoes'. I could hear clearly the bass notes of the model A playing the opening chords. After the band had finished their opening set, I was glad to sit down in my car and drive home after my fifteen hour day.

It was now high summer. I had spent the afternoon tuning various instruments in the dubbing theatres at Ealing Film Studios. A dubbing theatre was just like a normal recording studio with the addition of a cinema screen, where the images of the film would be projected. This was so the music could be recorded onto the film with perfect timing. I emerged into the sunlight after finishing at Ealing Studios and walked over Ealing common. Feeling hungry, I found a Pub and ordered a meal and a beer. I was now engaged in conservation with Christine. She had told me that she was a secretary for Hammersmith Council. Christine was several years older than me. We made a date for the following Sunday.

One Friday, at the beginning of August, I was booked by Maurice to tune an upright piano. Maurice had asked if I could help out with the delivery, stay for the function and help out with the piano afterwards. I asked Maurice "Where is the venue?" he replied, "H.M.S Belfast". We pushed the upright piano up the walkway, onto the Second World War cruiser, moored on the South Bank of the River Thames, just above Tower Bridge. Once inside the ship the piano was positioned. As I tuned the upright, people were getting food and drink ready for the occasion, for this was EMI's launch party for Chase and Dave.

While attending a recording session, for Peter Skellern at Mayfair Studios, I was sitting in reception having a coffee. There was the studio manager. He was talking about the new house he had just moved into. I said, "I wished that I could buy a house". He reached into his pocket and pulled out a business card and said "Ring this man". At the next opportune moment I rang the number on the card. The name was Lewis Ruskin. I told the man that I had been given his card by the manager of Mayfair Studios and that I would like to buy a house. The man asked what I did for a living. I told him about myself and that I had not been self-employed for very long. His next enquiry was about my earnings. I told him of the several recording studios I regularly visited and that I invoiced each one monthly. The man then asked me to get a copy of my earnings, together with a letter from each of the studios who employed my services, to confirm in writing, the average amount I earned each month. All of the studios obliged my request. When all the paper work was gathered together I took them to Lewis Ruskin's office in the Edgware Road. As I entered the address, there was a polished brass plaque, it read, 'Lewis Ruskin, Solicitor'. I pulled out my papers and handed them to him. He read through all of the letters of confirmation. He then looked up at me and said "Go and find a house". I was astounded at his statement. Within two months I was the proud owner of Twenty-six Hogarth Gardens, Heston, Middlesex. A spacious three bedroom, red brick, semi-detached house, gardens front and back. I had used the money I had saved from the sale of the model A Steinway as my deposit. The price of the house was twelve thousand five hundred pounds and my mortgage was with the Scarborough Building Society. On the mortgage agreement was the clause that I was not to let any of the property. I immediately let two rooms. One to my friend John and one to Mark, a young electronics engineer who worked for Maurice. I was now keen to find another Steinway. Unfortunately, I had very little funds. I asked Fred from Piano Transport if he knew of such an instrument. He told me that he had an old Steinway that was buried in his store. A few days later I had a call from Fred telling me he had got the Steinway out and on its legs. I made my way to Piano Transport's store in Finsbury Park. The six and a half foot Steinway was in the most deplorable condition. The case had been painted, coat after coat of black and white paint. Even the keys had been painted. Fred told me he had pulled the grand out of a Soho Nightclub called Night and Day. The only good thing about the piano is that it was complete, with its original legs, lyre and fretwork music desk. Fred said, "You can have it for a hundred pounds, and for that I will include delivery" We shook hands. I had the black and white piano installed in the back room of my new house. It was handy, as when I started to strip the casework, I could undertake this dirty job, outside the French windows in the garden. After applying stripper, coat after coat of scraping, as I broke through to the original rosewood, I could see there were hundreds of small indentations in the wood. It was when I pointed the marks out to Christine, she realised what the marks were. The indentations were from people dancing on the lid of the piano wearing stiletto heals.

I was now looking after a nineteen fifties Bösendorfer Imperial. The piano had been purchased in Switzerland by Chris Squires, the bass player from the band Yes. The instrument had been delivered from Switzerland and installed in Chris Squire's large thatched house, buried deep in Virginia Water. On my first visit to tune the Imperial, I was fascinated, for it had retained its original, hand finished, ebonized casework. This finish had, in my opinion, a far superior lustre than the modern spray finished polyester. There had been a sale of a new seven foot four Bösendorfer and I was to make my way to Gloustershire directly after its delivery. The remote old house was in a deep down wooded valley. The outside barn had been converted into a recording studio for Mike Oldfield. After I had attended to the piano Mike Oldfield asked if I could tune the piano in the future. We exchanged telephone numbers.

Another regular out of town tuning job I was attending to was for Pete Townshend. He had bought yet another Bösendorfer grand, for his home and studio, way up the River Thames at Goring. Pete had a state of the art new house built. It was made entirely of wood and glass. In the grounds of the house were a number of out buildings, which had been converted into a studio. I think Pete liked the banks of the River Thames.

One day I was working in a studio tuning the acoustic piano when a man dressed in a red and black, horizontally striped jumper, just like Denis the Menace, came in with various key-

boards, along with a number of amplifiers. He introduced himself. His name, Peter Webber. Peter said he had never come
across a young piano tuner before. He thought all piano tuners
were old. I told Peter I tuned Fender Rhodes and Clavinets etc.
He then told me he lived in Hounslow. I told him that I lived,
just up the road in Heston. Peter asked me if I could tune some
of his keyboards. Some days later I paid a visit to Peter's house.
On my arrival Peter was lifting a large amplifier out of the boot
of an enormous American car, which was full of band gear. I
gave Peter a hand into his house, with the amplifier. As we got
through the front door there was hardly room to move, for in
his hallway was a Hammond B3 organ with two Lesley speakers,
amplifiers stretched all the way up the staircase. Peter was running his embryo hire company from home, using his huge car
for deliveries. As Peter and myself had a cup of tea he told me
he came from Brixham, in Devon, and he used to live in a box
on the side of the harbour. He then told me he had toured with
the Nashville Teens in the Sixties, along with Dave, Dee, Dozey,
Beaky, Mick and Titch. He had left the music business for some
time and had taken up being a ranger on Wimbledon Common,
and now he was having another go in the music business. It was
handy for Peter being so close. He would often come round to
my house and unload keyboards for tuning. Also, Mark, being
introduced to Peter, was undertaking electronic repairs. Pat
from the Rubettes, regularly called by, as did a new client, Tex.
Tex was a colourful character and in his thick northern accent
he would always say, "Got yer beans". This was his reference to
have I paid you. Tex regularly came round for keyboards to be
tuned. He looked after the gear for Genesis.

My house was now as much a workshop as a home. John
had moved out, not happy with the mess and the visiting hirsute music business people. I had kept my association with
Bösendorfers and regularly called in at 38 Wigmore Street to
tune the stock of instruments. On one such visit there were
two men going all round the building. The suited duo were

writing things down on their clipboards. I had picked up the information that 38 Wigmore Street had been sold and the new freeholders were the Prudential Insurance Company. The two men were intrigued and came over to watch me tuning. After introductions, they told me that they were from the Prudential's Estate Office. I asked them what their intentions were for the basement. As they had not visited the area I led them down the spiral staircase. The two large basement rooms were dimly lit and filthy dirty. The two men walked around and took notes. Then one of the men asked me what my interest was. I told them I was possibly looking for a workshop. He then enquired, "For what purpose?" I told the two men, "For the repair and maintenance of pianos". One of the men jotted down my details. The following week I received a letter from the Estates Office of the Prudential. It read "Dear Mr Lowe, after meeting you at 38 Wigmore Street, The Prudential could offer the two basement rooms, on a twelve year lease, and the terms would be three hundred and ten pounds a year, including electricity and heating, to be paid quarterly in advance. If you would like to take up the offer please reply in writing". Christine typed my letter of acceptance. I signed the simple lease, paid three months in advance and immediately started painting out the basement. I had Fred collect the stripped down Steinway from my house and deliver it to my new premises. Fred said "Tel, you gotta golden opportunity here".

Many of the concerts that I was tuning for were for the promoter Harvey Goldsmith, and now, Harvey was booking me direct. Harvey's office was just round the corner in Wellbeck Street and whenever he required my services one of his staff, Carol, Beth, Andrew or Harvey's stage manager would simply pop round to my basement to see if I was available. I always was. A confirmation letter would arrive by hand within the hour, along with a stage-pass, a car park pass and meal ticket. I had done my first job for Harvey Goldsmith direct in early September, various keyboards to be tuned at Empire Pool. It was for Alice Cooper and his "Welcome to my Nightmare" Tour.

By the end of 1975 I had become a house owner, with business premises in London W1, along with an ever increasing list of clients in the music business. I can remember pondering where all of this good fortune had come from.

THE HEAT GOES UP

I t may sound all very well, going to all of these venues, but the one thing that started to get to me was traffic jams. I tried motorbikes, a Royal Enfield 250, followed by a Royal Enfield 700 which had been converted to a chopper and a Velocette 500 cafe racer ending up with the ideal bike, a Honda dirt tracker, with a slightly buckled front wheel. On occasion I even used my Victorian ladies bicycle. This ancient machine had enormous twenty eight and a half inch wheels, no gears and rod brakes. One had to sit bolt upright riding it, and when passing a double decker bus, I was so high up, I could look straight in the eye of the passengers who sat on the lower deck. Speeding down the cycle path of the A4, I passed, with ease, the slow moving traffic.

Early in the New Year, Hugh, my new lodger moved in. He was a tape operator/engineer at Landsdown. I would get some good tips from Hugh on recording techniques, for I was now starting to make my own music. Recording tunes on my newly acquired two track, valve tape recorder. This trusty old machine, with its knob's and leavers, was of very high quality. I had bought the reel-to-reel from Mayfair Sound for the sum of twenty-five pounds.

It was a slow start to 1976, attending to any studio tunings and spending the rest of the day in my new workshop. Peter Webber had asked me if I could help him deliver a Fender Rhodes and tune it. Peter picked me up at my workshop and we headed north to Highgate. On arrival I thought the detached property, situated at the south end of Highgate Cemetery, looked like a dolls house. The thought was quite appropriate, for Peter's client was Lynsey de Paul. While I tuned the Rhodes, Peter chatted to the doll-like star. When I had finished, I asked if I could use the bathroom. Lynsey said it was upstairs on the right. As I came out of the bathroom I could see through the open bedroom door Lynsey's large round bed, and placed meticulously, in the middle of the red bedspread, was a pair of tiny, naughty knickers. I joined Peter and Lynsey drinking tea in the kitchen. Along one wall were horizontal plumbing pipes and rested on the top pipe was a fishing rod. Peter asked Lyndsey "Why have you got a fishing rod?" she replied, "Ringo bought me that, as I was always fishing for compliments".

I was in and out of studio two, Abbey Road throughout February, attending to any keyboard needs for 'Wings'. February 18th I was tuning the newly acquired American Steinway concert grand for 'Queen' at the Hammersmith Odeon. Freddy Mercury asked me, "What did I think of the piano?" I told him, "It's got a great sound, but in my opinion, the action was in need of being serviced and regulated". Freddy gave me the number of his office and asked if I could liaise with them for the undertaking of the job. March 5th, I waited outside, while the band was finishing their sound check at the Empire Pool. The volume was too much for me. The performer was Robin Trower.

I had been asked to tune Brian Ferry's piano at his house in Holland Park. When I arrived at the address, the door was answered by a beautiful American blond. It was Jerry Hall. She asked me in and in her Texan drawl, asked me, "Would you like a coffee?" Jerry Hall was relaxed and easy going, while Brian Ferry was stiff, walking around the room with an upright posture, one hand in his smoking jacket pocket. He made me think of

Noel Coward. I was now working mostly for rock, pop and jazz musicians. I had to take great care over my work, for many of these musicians had learnt to play using their ears and in doing so, had developed an acute sense of tuning. I was still covering Bösendorfer's classical concerts, as many artist's were now using the marque. I had picked up on the grapevine; Steinway were feeling a little threatened. For Steinway, being so powerful, could supply an instrument anywhere, anytime, whereas Bösendorfer, could not. Using this power, artists were made to feel insecure about using Bösendorfer, for Steinway would make it difficult providing an instrument when Bösendorfer's could not.

It was always handy, if possible, to fit in any tunings in the local area to where I was working. I had to tune at 1pm and 6pm, for a piano being used for the Kenny Everett show at Thames Television Studios, on the banks of the River Thames, at Teddington. A little distance away lived one of my regular clients, Justin Hayward of the Moody Blues, (nice little afternoon cash job!). On returning to Thames Television, while taking a break, a handful of the session musicians were having a jam. I loved the Latin jazz theme the virtuosi were improvising on. I was most impressed with an unassuming little guy, who was a roadie. He played the most fantastic South American jazz style flute.

At the beginning of May I had been booked by Harvey Goldsmith, at 1pm and 6pm, for six shows in a row. The venue was Wembley Empire Pool. The booking was for David Bowie. I remember the keyboard player. He was a bad mouthed loud American. I remember two distinct things about these shows. First was when I heard Bowie sing. I was impressed with the strength and dynamic of his voice, and at the same time the astonished look on the faces of the girls in the front row. My other memory was of the obnoxious keyboard player.

I had arranged with Philip, from Eden Studios, to accompany him to Yamaha's warehouse in Bletchley. We tried many instruments and we both agreed on the new piano for the studio. Another block booking by Harvey Goldsmith, was for May 19th to May 23rd, again I was asked to tune the piano at 1pm and 6pm. The venue was Earl's Court, the band was the Rolling Stones and the keyboard player was Billy Preston. On the first of these dates I was amused by the stage, as it was a flower. When I laid my fingers over the keys of the Yamaha grand, it was perfectly in tune. The Stones had just arrived after touring the USA. I had to take my hat off to the American piano tuner who had tuned the instrument last. I made out, as if to do my tuning, cleaned the keys and left the stage. To make the backstage area more comfortable, the floors had been laid with plastic grass. There was an assortment of caravans, and a bar. Chefs, dressed all in their whites were taking orders for food. I produced my meal ticket and made my order. The food was excellent, what a treat, twice a day for a week. On returning at 6pm and checking the Yamaha after the sound check, I was still in time for my evening feed. I was hanging around, when a motorbike turned up backstage. The pillion rider dismounted and took off his helmet. It was Mick Jagger. When the show started, the closed flower stage started to open. I left Earl's Court, leaving Mick Jagger strutting his stuff on the end of a petal.

After the Rolling Stones started their last Earl's Court show, backstage it was pay out time. One of the caravans was being used by Harvey and his accountant. People were being paid off, for their various services. When it was my turn to enter the caravan Harvey said, "How much do I owe you Terry?" I told him how much and handed him my invoice. Harvey's jaw dropped. I had noticed his reactions on previous occasions. I could never work out whether Harvey found my bill too much or too little!

May Bank holiday, Monday, another all day event at Charlton. Again, The Who were top of the bill. The bands that needed my services were The Sensational Alex Harvey Band and the

American band Little Feet. The band I enjoyed the most were not using any keyboards. They were the American country rock band The Outlaws. I remember standing on the side of the stage as they played. I looked around and everyone had a look of astonishment. Then I saw Harvey Goldsmith drop-jawed with amazement. The following day I drove down to Gloucestershire. I tuned Mike Oldfield's Bösendorfer. Then he asked if I could tune some other keyboards. There was a Fender Rhodes, double manual harpsichord, spinet and a replica of a clavichord, one of the earliest of keyboard instruments. The hours went by and I worked my way through the different keyboards. Eventually, I had to ask Mike Oldfield, "Any chance of a cup of tea mate?" he looked at me and went "Oh!", and without a word he turned away and walked off. Sometime later he returned with a cup of lukewarm insipid tea. I wish I had asked for a glass of water.

Throughout June the weather was getting warmer. Maurice had booked me to tune the little black Steinway. It had been hired by Van Morrison. The address was about five miles outside of Reading. As it was so hot, I decided to go on my motorbike. As I roared down the M4, the breeze cooled me down. If I went too fast, the buckled front wheel would start to go wibbly-wobbly, so I was restricted to fifty miles per hour. When I arrived at the lone detached house, the door was answered by Van Morrison. He showed me to where the piano was and I set to work. There didn't seem to be anyone there other than Van Morrison. He sat back in an arm chair, throughout, while I tuned. Having finished, I was playing a few chords. He asked me if I wanted a cup of tea and over that cup of tea, he was asking me about what type of music I liked. I told him I liked 'Yes', the conversation died.

I had heard rumours of a new keyboard that Yamaha had brought out. I had even been taunted that the new instrument was going to put me out of a job. When I finally got to see the new keyboard, all fears disappeared for the Yamaha electric piano had strings which had to be tuned.

It turned out to be another hot day for this year's Crystal Palace Garden Party. I had arrived early on stage, tuned the grand piano and a couple of other keyboards. On the bill were Barbara Dickson, The Chieftains, Jess Roden, Freddy King and Eric Clapton. I knew the Chieftains were on after Barbara Dickson and as I was not needed for the Chieftans, there was the chance of a break. I took the opportunity to go for a walk. I wandered off, away behind the stage where I found a beautiful lake. After finding a sunny spot to sit in, I started eating my sandwiches. I had noticed, movement, among the lilly-pads, on the surface of the water. I tore off a crust of my sandwich and tossed it in. I nearly jumped out of my skin when a huge fish jumped out and consumed my crust. I laid back in the sunshine, listening to the Chieftan's in the distance. I sensed their set was coming to an end and returned to the stage. I checked the piano, ready for Jess Roden. While doing so, I looked out over the crowd. I noticed a familiar figure, precisely sited between the PA system, a short distance in front of the mixing tower. The lone man seemed to pop-up at just about every outside event. He was commonly referred to as Jesus, for he was always dressed in a robe. It did not matter what band was playing he would dance all the way through. I was familiar with some of Jess Roden's songs as he and his band had been recording their new LP at Mayfair Sound. The band had done a couple of numbers and had nicely loosened-up, when they went into the song, 'Round Inner Circle'. I had made my way into the crowd and watching Jess Roden, sing and move, with the rhythm section gelling perfectly with the brass section. I enjoyed Freddy King and Eric Clapton, but the high spot of the day for me was Jess Roden.

It was high summer and I was to tune a pair of Bösendorfer's in unison, for the Bracknell Music Festival. The two pianos had been married together on a rostrum, inside a very large marquee. I arrived early and worked my way through the pair of pianos. I could feel the temperature rising dramatically. As I had not been booked to stand by, I left the marquee. I wondered how long the pair of Bösendorfers would stay in tune, in the rising heat. Throughout August the heat went up and the work slowed down. Always the daily studio tunings, most of which I managed to get round before the sun got too high in the sky. The calm was not for long. There were daily visits to Air Studios at Oxford Circus. Bryan Ferry was starting to record some new tracks. I was making many visits to Chris Squire's, Pete Townshend at Goring, Ramport and his private house piano. Every few days, back down the M4 to Mike Oldfield's. One manic day I tuned the Steinway grand at Landsdown Studios, then westwards to Gloucestershire, tuning the Bösendorfer and double manual harpsichord, leaving Gloucestershire, without a cup of tea. Dashing eastwards back down the M4 to Goring, tuning for Pete Townshend, where I did get a cup of tea and finally arriving at the Southbank, in time to tune a Bösendorfer Imperial for an evening classical piano recital in the Purcell Room.

At the beginning of September, I was tuning at Air Studios, when Marc Bolan came out of the control room. As he approached me I noticed he had become quite portly. He knew my name and using both hands to shake mine, he thanked me for tuning the grand. I found Marc Bolan absolutely charming. There had been some sessions in studio one at Air London and using the Bösendorfer concert grand was the Canadian Artist Geno Vannelli. His music was powerful, using both rock and classical influences.

Whenever possible, I would make my way to my basement workshop away from the heat. I was making progress with the old Steinway. As the instrument was so old, the rosewood veneer was so thick, I was able to sandpaper all the stiletto heel marks out of the lid. This might not be possible on a younger piano, as the veneer used on a modern instrument is paper thin. Jimmy, the shiner from Challens, had started the process of French polishing the casework. While we worked together, Jimmy would sing away, songs from the War and more up-to-date tunes from the musical 'South Pacific'. Working at a bench, together with other craftsmen, was my favourite kind of piano work. Jimmy failed to turn up for the next time we had arranged. I found out the next day, Jimmy had been taken ill and died. Jimmy's death was another sad loss. The old school of highly skilled piano men was thinning out dramatically. It was getting harder to find a first class French polisher. Few young men had served an apprenticeship in the traditional way of finishing the case of a piano, for piano polishers were looked upon as the crème de la crème of their trade. All new pianos from the late nineteen fifties onwards were finished under the spray-gun.

Scorpio Sound was on the ground floor of Euston Tower. The in-house piano was tuned once a week, but as autumn approached, I was making almost daily visits for the Wurlitzer electric piano, which I was spending my time on. The band Supertramp were recording and the Wurlitzer was a key part in their unique sound.

One recording session at Pye Studios, Marble Arch, I was finishing tuning the studio piano as the musicians for the session were arriving. I noticed a guitarist tuning his instrument. I could not believe my eyes, for the immaculately dressed musician was Burt Weedon. I, along with a whole generation, had learnt to play the guitar from Burt Weedon's, 'Play in a Day'.

One evening, at the latter end of October, there was a phone call for Hugh. After the brief conversation he said, "I have to go into the studio for a rough mix for the record company". Hugh's old mini had broken down so I said I would give him a lift. On arriving at Landsdown Studios, Hugh unlocked the door and we went down to the control room. First of all Hugh pushed the faders up, which had the drums. It was a simple fast, manic beat. Up next came the bass, followed by an electric guitar, with a strong fazed effect. Hugh had mixed the rhythm section, when he pushed up the vocals. I looked at him and he looked at me, and we laughed and we laughed. I had heard nothing like it. The band was 'The Sex Pistols', and the song, 'Anarchy in the UK'.

The last tunings of '76 were for a New Year Eve's party at the Talk of the Town. Who was performing? I failed to make an entry in my diary and I cannot recollect the memory.

1977

From the first day of the New Year, there was a frenzy of recording sessions. All of the studios I looked after were booked solid. I had also taken on yet another studio. The studio was Utopia. They had purchased a brand new model B Steinway. Fitting in all of my appointments was sometimes difficult. Just one hitch, a problem with a piano or just another traffic jam. I would sometimes leave home at 5am, so as to fit in all of my jobs.

The last week in February, I had been booked to look after Oscar Peterson's favourite Bösendorfer Imperial. He had asked if I could undertake the tunings for all of his performances. The first date was the BBC Television Centre. I had finished my work on the Imperial, when Oscar came in the studio. He greeted me with a big smile and an even bigger handshake. The next date to tune was at two-thirty and at six-thirty, for a live broadcast, from the Shepherd's Bush BBC's TV Theatre. The following day, two-thirty and six-thirty back at the Television Centre. Oscar's final concert was at the Royal Festival Hall. I had been booked to have the Bösendorfer ready for 2pm, and to be in attendance, throughout the afternoon and retune for the evening performance. Oscar thanked me for looking after the piano which was now known as the Oscar Peterson Imperial.

Landsdown Studios had now decided to buy a new Bösendorfer and on the day of delivery I had been booked to be there all day. Part of the soundproof ceiling had to be removed, revealing a skylight window. Fred from Piano Transport was in charge. First of all, the old model B Steinway had been taken off its legs and was ready to be removed. The only way to get the old piano out and the new piano in was by crane. The skylight had been removed and the crane driver lowered in his cable. Fred tied the Steinway, double checking every fastening. The Steinway rose up and was lifted out. About an hour later the new model 7ft 4in was being lowered into its new home. I was looking up at the piano, as it came through the skylight, when a sheet of plate glass fell from above missing me by inches. I felt the wind and a whistle as the plate glass impaled itself on the studio floor.

The old model B Steinway, which had been in the studio for over twenty years, had been played on hundreds of hit records going back to the late 1950's, when the studio was started by Dennis Preston and Jo Meek. Because of the model B's history, Ray Cooper, Elton John's flamboyant percussion player, had done a deal with the studio and purchased it. I had given Ray an estimate to fully restore the instrument. Fred delivered the model B to my workshop later the same day.

Within a week I had taken all of the patterns for the bass strings, hammers and wrest pins. All of the old strings had been removed and the iron frame lifted out of the casework. I had repaired any splits in the soundboard and I was now scraping off the old varnish. I had company in my workshop. Mick, who I had worked alongside at Steinway's workshop, was also now self-employed. He had just returned from India, where he had spent several months servicing pianos. Mick worked on the action, keys and dampers of the model B, while I took care of the re-stringing. I now had taken on, on a part-time basis, Ted. He had a full-time job working as a dustbin man. He worked the early shift, finishing by late morning. After lunch, he would arrive at my workshop and put on his apron. Ted cursed the piano industry for its mean wages. He said he could earn more on the bins. Luckily for me Ted said he always liked to keep his hand in.

I stayed on after tuning a Fender Rhodes, and one of the new Yamaha CP70's, at Wembley Empire Pool. It was for the 'Hotel California Tour' by the 'Eagles'. Their show was impressive. The next day I had to tune the grand piano in a Grosvenor Square Hotel. I sat and listened to the polished all American band warm up for the sound check. The singer was Gladys Knight. I was drop-jawed impressed when she started to sing. I had not heard a singer with so much presence in their voice.

The price I was charging for an average studio tuning was five pounds. With more work than I could cope with I increased my minimum charge to seven pounds fifty, and in some case's, I doubled my fee to ten pounds. I thought I might lose some customers, but this was unfounded as I gained even more clients, like the guitarist Alvin Lee. His studio was in his house, a crumbling old mansion, a short distance outside the town of Henley-upon-Thames. Another guitarist I was working for was Mick Taylor. I would call in to tune his upright piano. Mick Taylor would sit with his girlfriend on a pile of beanbags. The pair just sat there for the whole duration, watching me tuning. There was another studio in Chelsea, Sound Techniques. I had several tune and attend sessions there for Cat Stevens. He was a hard task master, having the most acute hearing. There was more work from another hire company ML Executives. Their warehouse and office was based at Shepperton Studios. ML was run by some of The Who's road crew.

The Rainbow, early June, it was getting close to show time and I was struggling to get all of the keyboards sorted. They were drastically out of tune. I just managed to finish tuning the Clavinet, when I was asked to leave the stage. The band was Bob Marley and the Wailers. Backstage was full of Rastafarians, and the air was thick with the pungent smell of marijuana. I made my way up the narrow staircase to where food was being served. I had never had home cooked West Indian food before. It was hot and delicious.

The day before Queen's concert at Earl's Court, there was the opportunity to carry out the work on the Steinway model D. I spent the whole day working on the instrument, while all around me, the road crew were assembling the PA and back-line. The day of the first show I checked the piano ready for the sound check. When I returned to tune for the show, Freddy said, "Terry, the piano's wonderful". Freddy mentioned he had bought a piano in a New York auction, and it would be delivered to his house in the next few weeks. Freddy asked if I could come and tune it. Freddy said that he would give me a call as soon as the piano arrived.

Freddy's grand had arrived from New York. I went to his house in Kensington, rang the bell. The door was answered by a woman. I told her my name. She replied, "My name's Mary. Come in." I followed Mary into the sitting room. As we entered Freddy stopped playing and greeted me with an excited hand-shake. He then started to stroke the piano saying "Isn't it beautiful". The baby grand piano was a Broadwood from the late 1920's. Many piano makers around this period had artists come from Japan to lacquer the cases of grand pianos. This high lustre finish was done in many different colours. Black, white, red, yellow and blue. Then the artist would paint Oriental scenes all over the casework. On inspection of the workings, I told Freddy it all looked in sound condition. I advised that the instrument was in need of a good cleanout and the action needed servicing. Freddy asked if the piano would have to go into my workshop. I told him it was not necessary, as I could do all the work in situ. Freddy then asked me to go ahead as soon as I could fit it in and to liaise with Mary as he was off on tour.

There was a Sunday morning tuning for Elton John at Sarm Studios. When I arrived I was amazed. Fred and the boys from Piano Transport had managed to install a Bösendorfer Imperial. They must have struggled, as the only access was down a nar-row staircase. Fortunately for Fred the studio decided to pur-chase the monster piano as they loved the sound of it.

Maurice would start to panic if he could not track me down, and to get round the problem he had got me an air call. This device worked on short wave radio signals. If I was summoned, the thing would go off, and one could just decipher, through the static that I was then to call Air Call HQ to receive the message. I used to get some funny looks when the device went of, for it sounded just like the police. Some summer days, after the morning studio run, I would return home, leave the Air Call on the kitchen side, change into old clothes, make some sandwiches and ride my old bicycle through the grounds of Osterley Park, where I would spend the afternoon by the lakeside fishing.

Ray Cooper was on a world-wide tour with Elton John and whenever he was in town he would make a visit to see the progress being made on his historic piano. Ray was so happy upon the completion of the Steinway he paid me on the spot. He then started looking at the old Steinway grand which was now completed. Ray asked, "If it was for sale?" I said "Yes" and told him the price. Fred delivered the model B to Ray's flat, a converted tea warehouse on the banks of the River Thames at Wapping. After I had tuned it, Ray asked me about my Steinway. A couple of days later he called me to say he would like to purchase it for his girlfriend. Ray also told me he had a Grotrian Steinweg grand and could I give him a price to restore it.

I attended to the work on Freddy Mercury's piano. The job took two days. Mary supplied tea and sandwiches and she told me Freddy would not be home until the New Year.

1978

Ray Cooper's grand piano had been collected from his house in Suffolk and I had started to work on the instrument. I had also started the restringing of a model K upright Steinway for Pete Townshend. There was no work to be done on the cases of the two pianos as they were in good condition. Mick, the Steinway technician had gone off on another piano job abroad, so I asked the freelance technician, Les Pearce, if he could do some work for me. We agreed an hourly rate.

The studio circuit was having a quiet period at the beginning of the year, but the gap was filled with more jobs from ML, at Shepperton. Frank Zappa was using the sound stage M. He wanted all of his keyboards tuned on a daily basis. I was making regular visits to Freddy Mercury's, he was playing piano for many hours a day, writing new songs. Pete Townshend's Steinway upright had been completed. I managed to combine the delivery of the upright, back to Twickenham, and the collection of a grand piano, from an address in Chiswick on the return journey. The English made piano was a Collard and Collard. The instrument had been inherited by Phil Collins and he wanted me to carry out a full restoration on the old grand. The Collard and Collard, being just short of six feet in length, had the most beautiful case work. Mahogany veneers had been cut into squares and glued down on the lid, and by using the grain of the wood, in such a way as to create an illusion, which when viewed from the keyboard it appeared as if the squares of wood gave an almost three-dimensional effect. It looked like the blocks were standing up on one another.

I was talking to one of the ladies on reception at number 38 Wigmore Street, when one of the attendants of the above offices, a Colonel Sholty, slammed a set of keys on the desk and said, "I am leaving. If anyone would like any of my artefacts, please take what you like". He raised his hat and said, "Goodbye!" By the time he was out of sight, myself along with the receptionist were in the lift. He had left his office door ajar. On entering there was a musty smell. Colonel Sholty apparently had the office for years. Inside was more like a sitting room. I helped myself to a round mahogany table, a set of drawers and an unusual brass table lamp. I carried out some small repairs to the table. The round top was made of one piece of mahogany and was four feet across. Ted, the polisher had showed me the rudiments of getting a shine. Slowly my house was getting furnished, from pieces I came across that needed a bit of work before getting a new lease of life.

One of the few private house tunings I took on was for Montague Cleeve. He and his sister lived in a grand old house on the perimeter of Wimbledon Common. Mr Cleeve was an elderly gentleman. He had been an army officer in the First World War. He and his sister were both very good players, having a pair of grand pianos married together in their gracious sitting room. Mr Cleeve had called me, not to tune the pianos, but to have a look at an upright piano he had acquired. My heart skipped a beat when I saw the upright, for it was so beautiful. The instrument was made by the French company Erard. Its elegant lines and every part of its mahogany case was inlaid with satin wood. Mr Cleeve told me the case was made in the Adam style. He had rescued the Erard from a Wimbledon girl's school. He then told me it was painted white. When the piano was collected he had it put in his garage, where Mr Cleeve's handyman stripped off the white paint, revealing this beautiful casework. Mr Cleeve remarked, "The piano had such a good tone". I asked him what he intended to do with it. We shook hands at four hundred pounds. This beautiful piano was in my sitting room within a week.

March 21st, I had a booking from Capital Radio. The occasion, the 1978 Music Awards, to be held at Grosvenor House, Park Lane. I was to tune before the sound check and at 6pm. The star cabaret was 'Manhattan Transfer'. The 'Stones' mobile had been brought in to record the evening's events. I knew Pete the fish, he looked after the Rolling Stones mobile recording studio. There were too many names there to mention. I spent most of the evening inside the mobile studio enjoying the great food, which had been sent out. I joined the party when Manhattan Transfer started. They were amazing. At the beginning of April, I was tuning daily the concert grand for 'Queen', at Pinewood studios. At the same time I was preparing keyboards for 'ELO', at Shepperton. On May 3rd I had to tune at 11.30am and at 6pm for Diana Ross, who was appearing at the London Palladium. The morning job was straight forward. At 6pm, it was hard to hear the piano above the noise of Diana Ross's entourage, of which there were a great many.

Early April I was managing to get lots of workshop hours in. Re-stringing the Collard and Collard grand for Phil Collins. Les Pearce was working on the action and keys. I would watch Les go through each process with meticulous precision. Les cursed the piano industry for its low pay. Les regularly said to me, "Don't do them up. Deal them!" Piano dealers could make enormous profits, paying skilled staff, low wages. Les and I were having a tea break, when Andrew, from Harvey Goldsmiths came down the spiral staircase. Andrew asked if I could tune Queen's piano at Wembley Arena on the 11th, 12th and 13th of May. The first of the dates was a Thursday. After the daily chore of studios I had an early lunch, arriving at the arena with ample time to go through Freddy's piano. The name Empire Pool was no more. A fresh paint job and now it's known as the Wembley Arena. Queen's concert grand had a hard life, being moved every few days, coping with cold nights vibrating on a lorry, then getting toasted under the heat of the stage lights, and it would just take one inexperienced, provincial, piano tuner to make the whole instrument unstable. When I was satisfied with the instrument, I drove home for the afternoon, returning at 6pm to check tune, ready for the show. Freddy always made a point of thanking me for tuning his piano.

The next job for Harvey Goldsmith was for six dates at Earls Court. A pre-sound check tuning and again before the show. The artist – Bob Dylan. Wednesday June 14th was the first date at Earls Court. I always allowed plenty of time preparing pianos and keyboards on the first day of a run of concerts. The back-stage caterers were excellent and after a superb lunch, I stayed and listened to Bob and his band go through their sound check. The security was much tighter than I was used to, even the stage passes were changed daily.

I had been booked by Harvey for an outdoor event at Blackbush Airfield, in Hampshire. It was very rare that I would take anyone with me to any of my engagements. On this occasion, Christine accompanied me. We set of down the M3 especially early, arriving at Blackbush. I had to leave Christine backstage while I worked my way through the keyboards being used by Joan Armatrading, Eric Clapton and finally Bob Dylan. I was asked to check all of the instruments prior to each set.

The stage was enormous and very high, even from my elevated view I could not see the end of the crowd. I do believe there were over two hundred thousand people there. The day went smoothly enough. After Dylan had started, Christine and myself left Blackbush before the inevitable traffic jams.

I tried, where possible, not to work on Sundays. Bösendorfers had especially asked me to attend to an Imperial grand which had been chosen by the American pianist Garrick Ohlsson for his Wigmore Hall recital, followed, the next day, at the Royal Albert Hall. I had to tune and attend this concert as it was going to be televised live for the BBC Proms.

The Collard and Collard grand for Phil Collins was now completed and Fred had delivered it to its new home near Guildford. I found Phil's house at the end of a country lane. While I checked over the piano, Phil unwrapped a new drum machine which had been brought out by Roland. Phil was quite excited by his new machine.

Ray Cooper's piano had been finished and delivered to his apartment in Wapping. It looked the part in Ray's bedroom, a proper boudoir grand.

I was fortunate in getting Phil Collin's and Ray Cooper's pianos out of my workshop, as the week after there was a fire at 38 Wigmore Street and the whole of the lift shaft had gone up in flames. Fortunately, there was no other damage. After inspection by the engineers we were informed it would take several months to repair the lift. Luckily, I had no pianos in my workshop.

George Martin had selected a new Bösendorfer, 7ft 4ins. The instrument had to be specially packed in an airtight container, for the piano was to be delivered, by ship, to the West Indies.

I was now relying on tunings only for my income. There were always any number of casual tunings, various restaurants around the West End. I tuned a piano upstairs in a Soho drinking club. The piano was next to the bar where the Madam, who ran the establishment, served her clients. The air was thick with smoke and the odour of alcohol. The Madam asked, "Would I like a drink?" I said, "I would like a cup of tea". There was a snigger from around the bar. I started laying the chromatic scale, when the Madam slammed her hand down on the bar and shouted, "Quiet!" The drinkers went silent. I gave the bar a few chords when I had finished, receiving a round of applause. As I put the panels back into the piano the Madam paid me cash, with a fiver tip.

On one of my regular visits to Air Studios, George Martin asked me what I was going to do now I had no access to my workshop. I said, "I would have to wait for the lift to be repaired", George then told me about the studio which he was building on the island of Montserrat, in the Caribbean. George said the new Bösendorfer he had bought was on its way there. I asked George, "Is there a piano tuner on Montserrat?" George replied, "No, would you like the job?" I laughingly replied, "It would be a bit difficult for 10 o'clock starts!" George looked at me and said, "I'm serious". I told Christine of my offer to go and work in Montserrat. She said, "You lucky thing". I thought about George Martin's offer. I was getting weary of the constant pressure of studio tunings. Not the job itself, but the driving in and around the capital, mostly sitting in traffic jams. It was while sitting in the slow, crawl home, westward on the A4, the wind, rain and autumn leaves were falling, I decided to give George a call. A meeting was arranged. At the beginning of October I received a letter from George confirming our agreement. I was offered the post of resident tuner and repairer of keyboard instruments for Air Studios, Montserrat. I accepted the offer, and now had to give all my clients, notice. Christine typed all of the relevant letters, informing all of my clients I would not be tuning pianos after the last day of November.

At the end of October, there were three nights at Wembley Arena. Rick Wakeman was back playing with 'Yes' and this time the band was performing on a circular stage, made in the centre of the Arena.

I let Chris Squires, the bass player, know of my decision to go to Montserrat. I was now passing on the telephone numbers of other tuners I would recommend. The last job of 1978, for Harvey Goldsmith, was tuning various keyboards at the Rainbow.

Three nights of Olivia Newton John. I watched her go through the sound check. She had come a long way since I had first seen her several years before. A frightened looking young girl about to make her first appearance on British television. Christine had moved in with me and she was to be looking after my house while I was away. Hugh had bought my MG Roadster. I spent Christmas in Devon, as always, getting off the train in Paignton, my Mother would meet me from the train and before going home she would march me up and down the beach saying, "Breathe and get that London air out of you".

TUNING IN THE SUN

The first day of January 1979, Christine dropped me off at Heathrow Airport. The weather was foul. Snow, wind and ice. I boarded the jumbo jet and was fortunate in getting a window seat. The two adjacent seats were occupied by two zany characters. The pair dressed in light-weight expensive suits. I watched them betting on the fall of the dice. Over the speakers the Captain informed us that there would be a delay as the plane was iced-up, and we had to wait for the de-icing machine. It was over two hours before we could take off. My two neighbours had never stopped gambling. It seemed they would bet on anything, even the colour of the air hostess's knickers. As the airplane started to taxi, the pair put their dice and playing cards away telling me they never gambled during take-off. The first island stop was Barbados where the gambling duo got off. There were several other island stops before arriving in Antigua.

As I left the plane I was greeted by a wall of warm air. I was informed that my connecting flight to Montserrat had left, due to the late arrival of my flight. I was not the only one stranded. I had met up with Geoff Emrick, who I recognised from Air Studios in London. Also there were the members of the first band to be booked in the new studio, The Climax Blues Band. British Airways had booked us into a nearby hotel for the night. The next day we all boarded a small, twin propeller aircraft and flew the short flight to the island of Montserrat. We were met at the airport by Dave Harris, the studio manager, who I also knew from Air Studios, London. The transport was limited to two old mini mokes. The band took priority. As we waited, Geoff and myself got talking to a man who had come to sort the air conditioning at the studio. It was coming up to midday and all three of us were melting in the heat. One of the mokes returned. It was a relief to feel the breeze in the open-topped little car. The hilly landscape was covered in lush greenery and perfumed flowers filled the air. On arrival at the studio, which on the outside looked like a building site although the inside was virtually finished, the control room had a smell of everything new. I went through into the studio and in its own sound proof booth was the Bösendorfer, on its side, still in its packing case. Geoff and I were shown to a bungalow, up on a hill, overlooking the Caribbean Sea. The first thing I did was to plunge into the swimming pool and cool off.

The bungalow that I shared with Geoff on Montserrat

As the sun was going down Geoff and I walked further up the hill to a much larger bungalow, where the band was staying. I was introduced to George; he was a local chef, employed by the studio to prepare the communal evening meal. By now the sun had set and the air was filled with the noise of insects and whistling frogs. Dinner was served on the veranda overlooking the sea. Fish bisque and lobster followed by the juiciest fruits I had ever tasted. On the walk back to our bungalow, the noise of the nightly overture of wildlife became deafening. There were no street lights and with only the moonlight to see by, we negotiated our way, trying to avoid the massive nocturnal frogs, some the size of a chicken. On our return, Geoff opened a bottle of Tequila. We sat looking at the night sky. I had never seen so many stars. On the first peak of daylight, the noise of the wild ceased and I managed to get a couple of hours sleep. I was forced to get out of bed by the rising temperature. It was just after 8am and Geoff was still in bed. I went into the kitchen where I found a woman. I said, "Good morning", she replied, in fast flowing, pidgin English, of which I did not understand a word. I asked her if she could speak more slowly. I finally got the gist, "She com in every mornin and did da cleenin!" She told me to, "Go and sit down by the pool" I was served egg, bacon and toast. As I ate my breakfast I observed a young boy cleaning the surface of the pool, which was covered with all sorts of brightly coloured insects and beetles. I felt a whizzing noise, turning my head I saw my first humming bird, hovering, just an arms length away, sticking its long pointed beak into the middle of a flower and then darting to the next.

Tuning bag in hand, I set off on the walk to the studio. As I meandered down the narrow lane, taking in the vista, I thought it looked like the coast line of North Devon, where the hills meet the sea. The difference here was the lush vegetation, humidity and heat. Here and there, wild goats grazed, exotic birds flew through the skies. I passed locals along the way, all smiling, saying, "Mornin!" the walk was over a mile. I passed more humble homes. Some were no more than a shack of corrugated metal sheets made in a small clearing among the palm trees. I noticed the occasional iguana tied up by its tail to the bottom of a tree. I received some strange looks along my way.

The locals I passed were all brightly dressed and everyone wore a smile. As I approached the studio, I could hear calypso music coming from the builder's radio. All the workers said "Mornin Man". I smiled back and wished them all "Good morning". I was relieved to get in the studio, out of the heat of the sun. Dave Harris and two engineers were working on the newly installed recording desk. After a chilled lemonade, I started to unpack the Bösendorfer, removing the entire wooden crate and taking it outside. When I had fitted the treble leg and the back leg, I needed help to lift the piano onto its feet. Dave and the engineers had gone off in one of the mokes, so I went outside and asked one of the builders if I could have help with the piano. Everyone within earshot said, "I'll elp ya mon". I said "Three of you will be enough". I asked the trio if they minded dusting themselves down and washing their hands. I explained that we did not want to scratch the casework. My helpers gasped at the first sight of the piano. I instructed them what I wanted them to do. We all took hold of the treble end and lowered the leg until it touched the ground. The three went into excited chatter, not one word could I understand. I then told them that the next part of the operation was the hard bit. I explained they had to lift the base end of the piano, off the floor and hold it while I fitted the leg. The instrument rose from the floor. My helpers all saying, "Tis eavy mon". The legs and the pedals fitted, I raised the lid of the Bösendorfer. I sat at the keyboard and hit some chords. The three men looked on, now in silence, eyes wide open. I asked them if they had seen a grand piano before. The three replied, "No mon". I thanked them for their help as they returned into the sunshine.

The instrument, after its long journey, was not just badly out of tune, it had almost dropped a semitone below concert pitch. I set to work raising the pitch, sweat started running off me. The air conditioning was still not working. I was concerned for the piano thinking it will take a lot of tuning until the instrument would become stable. It was some three days later the air conditioning had been sorted out, and in that short period of time, the shiny steel strings of the piano were showing signs of corrosion, due to the high humidity.

It was my first Sunday on Montserrat. Mid-morning, I was in the pool having a swim. Geoff was sitting on the terrace having a coffee and a cigarette. When floating in the air came the sound of a steel band. Geoff said it was coming from the Viewpoint Hotel. After I had got dressed, Geoff and I wandered down the hill. The Viewpoint Hotel was no high-rise, just a simple reception, restaurant and terrace bar around the swimming pool, the rooms, all detached like little cottages around the palm trees.

The steel band played on the terrace and all around the pool was humming with people. I was captivated, watching the barman taking a whole pineapple with a machete, skilfully slicing off the skin, and then putting the whole fruit into a blender. Geoff said, "That's how to make a real pina colada". On the occasions Geoff and I sat having a tequila night cap, we discovered we both had an interest in classic cars. He told me he had a 1950's Bentley. What we both had in common was leaving school at the age of fifteen and learning a musical skill. Geoff also told me about when he was working alongside George Martin, at EMI Abbey Road, recording the Beatles in the 1960's.

Early Monday morning I put my hands on the case of the Bösendorfer. It felt cool to the touch. I took out my tuning fork, banged it on my knee and to my horror the pitch had gone way over concert. I went into panic mode, pushing down the whole compass of the keyboard below concert pitch. I then hit each note repeatedly. I left it to settle and put my attention to the Fender Rhodes. Being of such a simple design and having no sound board to move about, this instrument was reasonably stable. I punched the Bösendorfer into submission. By the end of the afternoon, I breathed a sigh of relief for the band was to start working later that evening. The next day, the piano needed tuning and the pitch was stable. I sat in on the first sessions, carefully listening to the keyboards. After a few days I was happy with the piano and preferred to sit outside, for the volume in the control room was too much for me.

On Friday afternoon, while sunning myself, I noticed one of the builders walking off into the bush. A few minutes later he returned having slit the throat of a goat with his Machete. The goat was butchered, cut up and put into a large cooking pot over an open fire. Other workmen had wandered off collecting other ingredients, all of which grew all around. I asked what the dish was. "Goat Water" was the reply. Some hours later the men downed tools for the day and all tucked into their goat stew. I asked if I could try some. I was handed a bowl and a spoon and told to help myself. I had never eaten goat before. It was a strong flavour. Another local dish I had tried was mountain chicken. This dish was not chicken but frog. The back legs of the enormous frogs looked just like a chicken leg and tasted delicious. After a couple of weeks I asked Dave, the studio manager about my wages. He told me there was a problem getting money out of the UK and said he would see what he could do.

I had made friends with some of the locals, who I got on with very well. On the occasion I was allowed one of the mini mokes, my new friends would pile in and they would show me around the island. On one outing we climbed up to the perimeter of the volcano and peered down into the crater, seeing the odd plume of smoke and the air was thick with the smell of sulphur. Other times I was taken to deserted beaches, the black volcanic sand being so hot, one had to run into the sea. Occasionally, visitors would fly in to look over the studio. Being the bottom of the pile, I would have to vacate my room in the house and take up residence in a lean-to, alongside the swimming pool. There was no mesh on the door or window like in the main house. Whenever I had to stay there I was severely bitten by mosquitoes. At the end of February, the band flew back to the UK. I was getting a little tired of not having my wages. Again I was the last in line. One evening, over the evening meal, I brought the subject of money up, when Dave the studio manager got very angry with me. So I got angry with him. We reared up at each other. I told him I quit. I had my scheduled air tickets for the return to the UK. Having no money Geoff loaned me fifty EC dollars, about twelve pounds in sterling. There was a tax to pay on leaving Montserrat. I landed in Antigua with the equivalent of a fiver in my pocket.

The first "Selfie" – Montserrat, 1979

WHAT NEXT

Arriving home mid-March was a bit of a shock, for the winter was far from over. I spent the first week sat in my armchair, keeping the home fire burning. Word spread quickly of my return and the phone started to ring. The first thing that I had to do was to buy a car. I settled for a 1961 MG Magnette. The four seater sports saloon only had sixteen thousand miles on the clock, one owner and in as new condition. ML at Shepperton was the first of my jobs, going through the stock of keyboards for the hire company. Peter Webber had acquired premises, a couple of railway arches in Putney. Peter based his hire company in one of the arches and had made a rehearsal studio in the second. He had expanded his business and now had many keyboards for me to look after.

I did not go looking for work, enjoying a more leisurely pace. I had no interest in taking any studio tunings on a regular basis, only on the odd occasion would I oblige.

On a visit to Pete Townshend's in Twickenham, he told me, "The Who, were having the addition of a keyboard player" I asked Pete, "Who it was?" he replied, "Rabbit". In April, 'The Who', were rehearsing with Rabbit on stage M, at Shepperton Studios. I was making sure that all the keyboards were in tune and in unison. Rabbit's real name was John. He was a friendly Texan and easy to get on with. Peter asked me, "If I would like to come and look after the keyboards on some dates?" The first outing with The Who was off to the South of France for the Cannes Film Festival. I boarded the plane at Heathrow with some of The Who crew; Burger – he did the lights, Eddie – looked after Pete's guitars and Annie – he wired all the keyboards. The flight was filled to capacity and it seemed that most of the faces were famous. I had never been star-struck by any of the names I had worked for, but I was captivated when I glanced behind, for sitting in the outside seat on the other side of the plane was David Niven. He was impeccably dressed with his hands clasped on his malacca cane. On arriving at Nice Airport, the in-crowd were picked up by a cavalcade of limousines. A short while later the last Rolls disappeared. The airport became deserted, not a soul to the seen, not even a taxi. We waited for a good while when two Mercedes squealed in. Annie took the keys of one of the hire cars. The two Mercedes raced along the Cote de Azure all the way to Frejus. It was a hairy drive.

The rest of the afternoon was spent sitting around the pool having the crack with the crew. The sun was hot, so I topped up my tan which had still not faded. When I jumped in the pool I got a shock, it was freezing, not like in Montserrat. In the evening we drove down the coast to Cannes. The bright lights, the glitter and the flashing cameras. There was a lot of alcohol consumed and the boys got louder and louder. Sitting in one of the outside bars, they got a little bit out of hand taking the "Mick" out of everyone. We were asked to leave.

Crew call was at 9am the next morning. Not one of the crew was late. The stage had been erected in a Roman Amphitheatre, near Frejus. Everything had to be ready for the sound check at 5 pm. I went with Annie and sat down opposite the stage, half way up the original stone seats. Being the only people sat there, Annie and I had our own show of 'The Who'. At one point John Entwistle handed his bass guitar to Eddie, the guitar roadie, as the band played on John stepped down off the stage and walked around listening to the out-of-front sound. The evening meal was served. We ate alfresco.

When the sun had gone down it was time for the lasers to be focused. Carefully setting all the mirrors so the laser beams could be directed where wanted. Later we all descended on the bars of Frejus. The next day was a leisurely start, arriving on stage in the afternoon. I went through all the keyboards, all was well. The crew meal was at 7pm. As the light faded the auditorium filled to capacity. On the stroke of nine o'clock the lights went up and the first chords of 'Substitute' rang out. It was quite a sight seeing a Roman Amphitheatre with a roaring crowd filling the ancient venue. The Who did a repeat performance the next night and immediately after the band had finished the whole crew went to work, stripping down the gear and loading it onto the trucks. All the stage gear was first. Keyboards, drums and amplifiers. When Annie and myself had secured all the keyboards on the truck, we were finished. Next, the sound technicians and the roadies stripped down the mammoth PA. Finally the lighting crew could strip down their rig. All this completed, the trucks left on their journey to Paris. The next day was a day off. Always being an early riser, I left the crew, all still asleep, and decided to have a day out on my own. I walked around the town of Frejus, having lunch overlooking the Mediterranean Sea. There was another crew turn-out into Cannes that evening. The crew were on better behaviour. The next day was a recovery day. Everyone just hanging around the pool. The hotel served a specially prepared lunch of roast beef. We were up at 6am the next morning, leaving the hotel by 7am. The two Mercedes were handed in at Nice Airport, not in the condition they were picked up in. We checked in for our flight to Paris. The venue in the French capital was known as the 'Abattoir'.

The Yamaha CP 70 was in poor shape. Rabbit had pounded it at the last show. Then the five hundred mile trip vibrating on the back of the truck. It just took a little longer before I was happy. The show was over by 10.30pm, and then there was the crew boogie at Le Palace in Montmartre. The crew certainly let their hair down. There were many perplexed faces on the chic Parisians, who were not used to such goings on. I had sampled some very expensive brandy at the crew bash but had not over-indulged, so while the crew slept it off, the next morning I went exploring Paris. I found a piano shop. The establishment sold new and second hand instruments. There were brand new Playel uprights and grands. The salesman spoke no English and I no French. We communicated by gestures. I tried one of the Playel grands. The tone was not big, but so beautiful. I looked at the salesman and said, "Chopin!" he clasped his hands and said "oui, oui, oui". He seemed very pleased that I knew the Playel piano was the favourite of the composer. I had a look around the showroom when a man came through a door wearing an apron. The odour of French polish and the smell of the glue pot wafted around. The re-polished cases of older pianos were of an exceptionally high standard, so was the finish on the action and keys. But as far as the tuning of these instruments, I could have spent a week working on them. Showtime again at 9pm. After the last chords, it was stripped down and back to London.

A couple of weeks after returning from Paris, it was The Who's tour of Scotland and the two shows were in Glasgow and Edinburgh. The crew bus left Shepperton, on time, at 8am. The inside of the bus had been remodelled. Open plan lounge with video screen, a very loud sound system and blacked out windows. With no border controls the whole of the four days was an orgy of excess.

It was several weeks before the next time the band needed my services. I spent my time doing maintenance jobs on my house. I had acquired the smallest Bösendorfer grand, measuring 5ft 3ins. I had revived the instrument without having to restore it. This I did in my sitting room. Mike Oldfield had said he would like to try the piano. On giving him instructions on how to find my house, he was over an hour late having got lost. He arrived outside my front door in his shiny red Ferrari, accompanied by a very attractive girl. He played for a good hour before saying he loved the middle and the treble sections, but he found it lacking in the bass. He roared off in his gleaming sports car. I sold the little Bösendorfer to a private individual from the midlands. Money was getting a bit tight through the summer. I had pianos to tune for Todd Rundgren and Chase and Dave, at Knebworth on the 11th August. Then it was back with The Who, outdoors in Wembley Stadium. On stage by 8am, I set about tuning Rabbit's keyboards. I was approached by one of the road crew looking after Nils Lofgren. He asked if I could tune a couple of key-boards. I said "Yes, if you are paying cash". We agreed terms. I managed to fit in the welcome extra jobs and all was ready for the ten o'clock soundcheck. The stadium was filled to capacity, when first on Nils Lofgren, started his set. On the stage was a small trampoline and now and again he would take a flying jump, bound into the air and do a back flip while still playing his guitar. Nils thanked me personally, giving me a signed copy of his new album. Next on was AC/DC, followed by The Stran-glers and finally at 8pm, The Who. The lights and lasers looked spectacular. There had been a warning from the GLC about not lowering the laser beams over the crowd. This safety issue was ignored and the GLC ordered the lasers to be switched off half-way through the show.

A week later, the troupe travelled to Nuremberg, in Germany. Arriving late evening we checked into the hotel. Early next morning I was on stage, which was immense, all ready by 9am for the sound check. This went on like a military exercise throughout the day. Listening to the different bands, I went for a walk around the venue which was an old Zeppelin field. It was used by the Nazis for enormous parades coming up to the Sec-ond World War. I had ignored the notice in the hotel room, 'Not to open the windows at night'. The next morning I opened my eyes and to my disbelief, the whole of the ceiling was alive with insects. Just at that moment there was a banging at my door, Annie was shouting "Get up Terry, we can earn some extras". I replied, "What do you mean, we?" I escaped my invasion of insects and, without breakfast, I was being driven by Annie at high speed towards the gig. She was telling me that the first band on needed their piano tuned. There was a wailing of a siren and we were brought to a halt at gun point. A machine gun was pointed through the window of the Mercedes. I just sat still and said nothing. Annie managed to explain we were needed on stage. Obligingly, we had a police escort for the rest of the way. I started tuning a Yamaha CP 70 for the first band on, a German band called Zanki. With little time, I was speeding through the tuning. As I looked out over the crowd, directly below the stage were hundreds of American soldiers. They must have been there for hours to gain their prominent position. The sound engineers were sending the noise of me tuning through the PA. I was not far from finishing when a beer can hit me on the side of the head, followed by another. After getting showered with cans by the GI's, I left the stage in a hurry. Zanki started the day at 10.45am. As the band played, I tuned Nils Lofgren keyboards using headphones. After the Nils Lofgren set, it was time for the Steve Gibbons Band, followed by the Scorpions, AC/DC and Cheap Trick. The next tuning I had to do was for Miriam Makaba. As she played her African songs, which were appreciated after the high energy afternoon, I checked Rabbit's keyboards and at 8pm, The Who went on.

I had to bill the German promoter for the three extra tunings. Having worked out in Deutschmarks the fifty pounds for each tuning, I entered the promoter's backstage caravan. I was surprised, for he looked just like a fair haired version of Harvey Goldsmith. He raised his head and said in German-accented English, "How much do I owe you?" I told him "A hundred and fifty pounds", unlike Harvey's dropped jaw, there was no reaction, so without a thought I said, "Each!". He counted out the equivalent of £450 in Deutschmarks. I left the caravan a little drop- jawed. 'The Who' finished at 10 pm. By 11.30pm the gear was on the truck. The crew had got wind of my extra earnings and I was jibbed into buying all of them a drink in the hotel bar. I told no one about saying "Each!" to the German promoter.

I was home by early September and went back to casual piano work. The lift at 38 Wigmore Street was still out of action. I could gain access to my basement workshop by the spiral staircase, using the space as a West End hang-out. My income fluctuated after giving up my steady round of studios and without a regular income I decided to have a valuation done on my house. After two local estate agents had visited, both giving me the same valuation, £39,500.00. I still owed £9,000.00 on my mortgage. I started looking for property under £30,000.00. Wherever I went tuning pianos, I would look in any estate agents windows within the vicinity. After tuning Pete Townshend's piano, in Twickenham, I went on a wander looking in different estate agent windows. Most of the properties in Twickenham were too expensive. Then I spotted a terraced house for sale in Clapham. I thought that was strange seeing a house for sale in Clapham and being advertised in Twickenham. Entering the estate agents, I asked for the details, questioning the receptionist, "Why was a Twickenham estate agents, selling a house in Clapham?" She informed me, the house had been left to the present owners, an elderly couple living locally in Twickenham. They had asked us to sell the property with "As little fuss as possible". Arrangements were made to view the house. The address was Leathwait Road, Clapham. Arriving an hour before the estate agent, I viewed the property. The red brick terraced house had several steps up to the front door, iron railings bordered the front of the house with a gate leading down to the basement. The self-contained basement flat was occupied by an elderly lady. The estate agent arrived and opened the front door. The two ground floor rooms, had ornate high ceilings. The first room I entered had a fireplace made of black marble. There was a bay window, which looked out to the front of the property. The main sitting room was enormous, with its white marble fireplace, the shoulder-high mantle piece supported a gilded mirror, rising up some four or five feet, with cupid's meeting at the top. The bay window was big enough for a grand piano and looked out into the small walled garden. The staircase was wide, with a heavily made mahogany banister. On the first floor were the kitchen and two other rooms, both with bay windows. The next floor there was two more rooms and the bathroom. There was a reduced sized staircase leading to, two, very large attic rooms. From the first floor, and above, the view from the rear of the building was unobstructed looking out over the common. The agent informed me the building seemed to be in good structural condition, although the roof needed work. He also told me, the identical house next door had been converted into four self-contained flats. We descended down the outside steps to the basement. I was introduced to the elderly occupant. She showed us around. The kitchen had the original Victorian range. I had a brief look around, thanking the old lady for showing me her home. I liked this house. There was loads of space, beautiful rooms, although in need of redecoration, everything was in good condition. I asked the estate agent how long the property had been on the market. He told me, "Not yet one week". I had a bit of a sleepless night thinking of the house in Clapham. By 9.30am the next morning I had instructed both estate agents to market my house. I rang the agents in Twickenham and offered the asking price of twenty-thousand pounds, subject to contract for the house in Clapham. I delivered my confirmation in writing to the agent.

At the end of September I had a call from John Hamil, the road manager for Wings. I met up with John and he told me that Wings were going out and wanted to take a grand piano on the road. John asked if I was interested in doing the tour. I asked him what the money would be. He said, "How much do you want?" A mutually acceptable figure was agreed. John asked about hiring a grand piano and I suggested a Bösendorfer. The arrangements were made and I started work for Wings, on the 22nd October. It was the first time I cancelled bookings taken from Harvey Goldsmith, dates from around the UK, with Queen and the UK tour with ABBA. Fred delivered the Bösendorfer 7ft 4ins to a theatre in Eastbourne on the south coast. Paul and Linda lived just a few miles away and did not want the daily commute to a London rehearsal space. So the theatre, not being used in the winter, was rented for the duration, preparing to take Wings on the road. Shortly after Fred had left, I tuned the grand. Wings road managers John and Trevor arrived, followed by a truck load of gear. I was introduced to two more members of the crew. Wad the drum roadie and Bill, he was an electronics expert. Everyone mucked in unloading the drums, amplifiers and Linda's keyboards, which consisted of a Fender Rhodes, double manual Mellotron, Elka string machine and a mini moog synthesiser. I was checking the pitch of all these keyboards while the set was being built, elevated drum rostrum and behind the drums a platform for the brass section. The grand piano was centre stage.

The crew were booked into the Grand Hotel Eastbourne. Over dinner we all got to know one another. The next day everyone made an early start. My first job was to fit the pick-up to the grand. I took most of the day fitting the magnetic pick-ups, covering the whole compass of the keyboard. A lead from each pick-up was wired into a mixer, each pick-up having its own volume control. I had to carefully balance the sound. At the end of the second day, the PA and on-stage monitors had been installed. All was ready for the arrival of the band. Noon the next day, Steve the drummer arrived, along with the guitarist, Laurence. Denny Lain arrived. Paul and Linda had driven their personalised Wood and Picket customised Mini. There was an hour of everyone getting to know each other. Cups of tea and having the crack. Then Paul said, "Right girls. Time to get to work!" the first song was a Beatles cover, 'Got to Get You into My Life'. As the band worked their way through the set list, Paul would occasionally stop playing, giving instructions to the band. No one song was dwelled on for too long, throughout the afternoon and into the evening the set finished with 'Band on the Run'.

My daily routine, after having a silver service breakfast in the Grand Hotel dining room, would consist of a walk along the promenade to the theatre. I was usually the first to arrive, using the quiet time to make sure everything was in tune.

By the end of the week the band had really started to gel. Going through the numbers with a good flow. Friday night it was everyone home for the weekend. Everyone returned on the following Monday, with the addition of the four players making up the brass section.

Some days Paul and Linda would bring their children, who were looked after by the Nanny. Having little to do while the band rehearsed I made Stella and James a life size robot. Lots of fun was had cutting up old cardboard boxes and taping them together to form our model.

One morning I was playing the piano when two of the American brass players joined in. The trumpet player got behind the drums and the sax player picked up an electric guitar. I was playing a simple progression of jazz chords. The two went into virtuoso mode, improvising all around my chords. I had not the ability to play anymore and when the jam fell to bits, one of the players said to the other, "You like this guy, he leaves spaces".

A couple of weeks in, there was a day's outing. Everyone on a coach. We were driven to a country pub which had been booked for the whole day and night. This was for filming the Christmas video 'Having a Wonderful Christmas Time'. The producer told us all to eat, drink and be merry. So we did. After hours and hours of take after take, the producer said "It was in the bag!" We all had a good sing song on the way back to Eastbourne.

With the expertise of Ru, my solicitor, the drawing up of the contracts for the purchase of the house in Clapham, was in slow mode. I was getting a little anxious, as the agent in Twickenham had called to ask, "Why there was a hold up?" One of the agents acting for the sale of my house told me that there was a lot of interest but no offers yet. Calling the second agent, he informed me that one couple had asked for a second viewing. I was home for the weekend when a call from the agent saying an offer had been made on my house. The agent told me that it was for £37,500.00, some two thousand pounds below the asking price. The agent added the couple making the offer were cash buyers. I accepted the offer and asked Ru to go full speed ahead.

Returning to Eastbourne on Monday morning, another week's work passed by, everyday the band going through the set. There were fewer stops made by Paul. One afternoon, during a break, I was checking out the grand piano. Paul asked me about the balancing. I was trying to explain when Paul snapped at me and said, "Don't get technical with me Terry!" I made no reply.

With the luxury lifestyle staying in the Grand Hotel for a month, I had gained a few pounds, so I now ran the mile from the hotel, along the beach to the theatre.

John Hammel looked after all the guitars for Paul and Denny. I would help John change some of the strings on some of the instruments. I could play Denny's guitars, but not Pauls being left handed. John handed me Paul's Hofner violin bass. I was probably holding one of the most famous guitars in the world. Sellotaped to the rim of the bass was one of the last set lists the Beatles played.

During an afternoon break, I was having a cup of tea talking to the out-front sound engineer. I sat in front of the mixing desk half-way up the stalls. Paul was on the stage. Linda and the kids had sat down a couple of rows back from the front seats. Paul picked up his Gibson six string electric guitar and proceeded to go through a medley of early Beatles love songs, never looking away from Linda and their children. I will always treasure listening to Paul sing those songs, I had never seen the Beatles live. This was the next best thing.

The piano was holding up well. I purposely went and sat out front, listening to the set, which was now honed and polished. I was happy with the sound when Denny played the grand singing The Moody Blues hit song, 'Go Now'. Paul sat at the keys and sang 'Fool on the Hill' and 'Let it be'.

For the last rehearsal, the warm-up act went through his gags. His party trick was to impersonate the sound of a saxophone, using only his voice. A lone piper dressed in the full regalia, kilt, sporran and knee-high socks stood over the brass section playing the bagpipes to 'Mull of Kintyre'.

I was in the green room having afternoon tea, when I received a phone call from my solicitor telling me that both the contracts, for the sale of my house and the purchase of my new home, were ready to sign. I put down the phone and excitedly said out loud, "I've got my new house" Linda said, "Great Terry, where is it?" I replied, "Clapham". Linda said, "Chobham?" I repeated, "No, Clapham" Linda turned her head and pulled a face saying, "Errr". I thought to myself, "If I had your money, I could buy a house in Chobham".

The gear was stripped down and on its way to Liverpool, ready for the first date of the tour. I had two days in London, signing both the contracts, for the sale of my house and the purchase of my new one. Wings' road crew caught the train northwards. We all checked into the Holiday Inn Liverpool. There were to be three nightly performances at the Liverpool Royal Court Theatre. While in his hometown Paul threw a party for his family and friends. Even at this private function Paul was in the limelight, with a film crew documenting the event. The morning of the first show I made use of the hotel's swimming pool, sauna and jacuzzi. The first show went without a hitch. The folk of Liverpool welcoming back their local hero. The second and third shows everything ending in a standing ovation. Next it was off to the Manchester Apollo for two nights. Queen, were in Manchester at the same time and we managed to catch the end of one of their shows. Later, backstage, Freddy shook my hand saying, "Terry, my piano misses you".

December 1st one show at the Southampton Gaumont. The numbers were flowing. I always positioned myself behind Linda's keyboards, peeping out at the audience was always a sight to be seen. The people in the front rows, their faces beaming at seeing the former Beatle. The penultimate song was 'Mull of Kintyre'. The piper just faked playing as the sound of the bagpipes came from the Melletron. The spotlight went up on the lone piper, just at that moment there was a fault. I heard the sound of the pipes had gone way out of tune. Linda was oblivious. Paul turning around telling her to stop playing. I felt helpless, there was nothing I could do. After 'Band on the Run', the last number had finished, backstage, Paul put everyone on the spot. A new Melletron was ordered, ready for the next night at the Brighton Centre. As the band started to play, a buzz developed. The irritating noise was coming through the onstage monitors and the out-front PA. When the band was in full flow the buzz became inaudible. Everyone was checking equipment where possible. Paul being the true troubadour went from one song straight into the next.

There was a showdown. No one was going anywhere until the fault was found. Bill, the electronics expert, checked all the gear, telling all the crew "Not to touch anything!" I felt a bit uneasy, hoping the fault was not coming from the piano. The fault was finally diagnosed. It was Denny's new guitar amplifier. The Piper failed to show up for the next night in Lewisham. Wad, the drum roadie, was dressed in the pipers outfit and saved the day. After the shows in Southeast London I managed a couple of days at home. I wasn't feeling too good and spent a day in bed. The next morning I felt worse and visited my Doctor. After he examined me, I was told to take some aspirin and rest. It was the flu.

During the performance at the Rainbow, I was feeling really ill. I managed to strip down the gear and load the piano on the truck. Instead of returning to the crew hotel I took a taxi home. The next morning I felt even worse, revisiting my Doctor he repeated his diagnosis "It's the Flu, go home and rest". Throughout the day my head felt like it was splitting in two. By the evening, I had become delirious. Christine called an emergency doctor. After he checked me out, I was rushed into Charing Cross Hospital. I could not stop being sick until I was just bringing up bile. I was put into an isolation ward with suspected meningitis. After a lumbar puncture, meningitis was confirmed. I asked Christine to call Harvey Goldsmith's office and let them know.

The condition deteriorated. The pain in my head felt like my skull was going to explode. I could not stand any bright lights and I started to hallucinate. Some ten days passed before I started to feel conscious. The first visitors were mum and dad. They had come from Devon to help with moving, as the completion dates on the properties coincided with the time I was non compos mentis. Day by day, I felt a little better. I had many flowers and cards wishing me well. I had a generous bunch from Harvey and his staff, all signing the card, there was nothing from Wings. After two weeks in the hospital bed, I was allowed to have a bath, what joy! I had a final check-up by the doctors giving me a lecture about having time off work and taking regular holidays.

I left hospital, spending Christmas and New Year in Devon, recovering from the illness. By the beginning of January I was feeling much better, although week and fragile. I telephoned John Hammel. He was surprised to hear my voice. I told him of my illness. John said that he did not know that I had been in hospital. The band thought that I had done a bunk off the tour because of moving into my new house. I told John that I would not be coming on the rest of the tour as I felt too weary. The day after I returned to the Southeast, I heard on the news Paul McCartney had been jailed for bringing marijuana into Japan; it was the end of Wings.

For a few weeks I stayed with my sister at her house in Farnborough. It was a slow process regaining my strength. Wrapped up in a new cashmere overcoat, I drove the car into London making a first visit to my new home. On arriving at Leathwait Road, I knocked on the door of the elderly tenant in the basement flat, letting her know of my plight. On entering the house it felt very cold. All of my belongings were here. The Erard upright piano had been put in the elegant sitting room. I sat and played a few chords. After climbing the staircase and looking around, I felt exhausted. I managed to make a cup of tea and sat down in the armchair in the rear first floor bedroom, staring over the treetops, I went into a dream-like state, reminiscing over the past ten years. My feet had hardly touched the ground. I thought of the time I had been tuning concert grand pianos in the Royal Albert Hall, being the only person in the cavernous auditorium. I had tuned many times on various film sets when Lindsay Anderson was directing, always dressed in the same leather jacket. He would give me the most intense stare as I worked on the piano. On stage, tuning a grand piano, I looked up and there was Ertha Kitt. I couldn't help but smile. Then she looked at me and gave me one of her famous growls. I beamed even more. Late one afternoon, returning home from a gruelling day, made harder as my car was in for a service, the phone rang, it was the tour manager for 10cc. He asked "Could I get to Hammersmith Odeon as soon as possible, as the Fender Rhodes was out of tune?" I told him, "My car was out of service and that I couldn't get there before the show", he said, "We will send a car for you". A Rolls Royce, just like the Queen rides around in, pulled up at my front door. Tuning bag in hand, I sat in the back seat of the limousine, as we sped off towards Hammersmith. I found the keyboard in tune. One of the band said, "Between C and E was oscillating". I put my hand on my forehead and said "It's supposed to". He must have heard the beats of a major third for the first time. I got paid in cash, returning home in the chauffeur driven Rolls Royce. I would have the odd call from Tittenhurst Park, and on one occasion I had to go and tune the white piano in the middle of the night. I nodded off with these memories flowing through my head. On my awakening, my tea, half drunk was cold. I returned to the kitchen. While waiting for the kettle to boil I looked up at the ceiling. There was a large crack in the plaster. I prodded the crack with the broom handle when the whole of the ceiling came down, hitting me on the head and covering the kitchen with debris. In an instant, I said to myself "Sell-up and move to Devon".

I placed an advertisement in the Evening Standard saying, 'For Sale, Large Victorian Terraced House, offers in the region of £40,000.00'. I was inundated with calls. Eventually I accepted an offer of "£45,000.00 made by the sixties pop artist David Oxterby.

My mother started sending me the property sections from the Western Morning News. While contracts were being drawn-up for the sale of the house in London, I viewed many properties in Devon, finally having an offer accepted for a house in the village of Chulmleigh.

RETURNING TO DEVON AND LEAVING THE RAZZAMATAZZ

My new village house was of an unusual design. The ground floor and external walls had been built in 1827 and one hundred years later, in 1927, a first floor colonial style bungalow, four bedrooms, two reception rooms, kitchen and bathroom was built on top of the solid granite walls. To the front and rear, balconies with overhanging eaves stretched the whole length of the building. The rear of the property was a large walled garden. The ground floor, other than a utility room, was one open space which was to become my new rural workshop.

Christine had aspired to being the personal assistant for the chief executive of the Royal Borough of Kensington and Chelsea. She had given in her notice and we started our new life together in Devon. We set about redecorating our new home. I made a new kitchen using planks of oak found in the workshop. A new bathroom was installed and finally, new fitted carpets throughout.

The first piano to arrive for restoration was from Tony Banks, the keyboard player from 'Genesis'. The old, model A Steinway needed everything to be done. Although I could do all the work myself there was a problem. I could not refinish the rosewood case. Knowing a good French polisher was hard to come by, I looked through the Yellow Pages. One advert caught my eye, 'JOE BARTON. THE PARAGON FRENCH POLISHER'. I rang the number asking if I could have an estimate for re-polishing a grand piano. After giving him my address, he said, "You are only a few miles away. I will come and see you after lunch". In the afternoon he looked over the casework of the Steinway asking, "What finish I wanted?" Joe told me he had moved from Kent to Devon the previous year and that he spent most of his time re-pairing and polishing furniture for the antiques trade. He then said, "If he was to undertake the job, all the parts that could be removed he would take to his workshop and he would make visits to polish the rim of the case". I asked him for a price. When he gave me his figure, I thought to myself, "That's reason-able". I, not knowing the standard of his work, decided to take a chance. Five weeks later the job was complete. I was relieved and delighted for Joe had done a first class job. The rosewood case glowed. Joe was soon to work for me again.

Word travels in rural communities. One day there was a knock at the front door. The man, dressed in country tweeds, asked me, in his Devon accent, "Are you the piano man?", he told me that he had a Steinway grand, and that his son studied at the Royal College of Music and wanted the piano tuned. The gentle-man farmer drew me a map of how to find him. This job was to be my very first tuning in Devon. Having found the remote farmhouse, I set about my task. The Steinway model B was a good piano. Just as I had finished the last note, the man intro-duced me to his son. I stood up and asked him to try the piano. The young man played very well and after ten minutes he stopped, looked straight into my eye and said, "You're wasted here".

Christine had secured a new job in the market town of Tiver-ton, some eighteen miles away and was commuting daily. I had placed an advert in the North Devon Advertiser – 'Pianos. Tuned and Repaired. Pianos. Bought and Sold. Chulmleigh 232', the phone started to ring. I took on a local lad, Lesley. At first, I found him hard to understand, speaking in his thick Devon accent. I purchased an old Bedford ambulance and we started to collect pianos I had bought, soon filling the workshop with all makes of pianos. Lesley took to the job, buffing keys and polishing brass work. Soon I had a small stock of pianos for sale. One day, after loading the back of the Bedford with lead found in the back garden, I took it to the local scrap yard. While the lead was being weighed, I spotted an old cast iron glue pot, rusty, but in perfect condition. I asked the scrap man, "How much?" he replied, "You can have it for a pound". On the first boiling up of glue, Lesley said "What a stink".

My house in Chumleigh with workshops and private walled garden, early 1980s

A friend from the music business called me. He told me, he was now the road manager for Duran Duran and one of the band wanted a white baby grand. I found a suitable instrument for sale. The small Broadwood grand had been in the local grammar school for years. The case was in awful condition after years of school children scratching their names into the casework. As I was looking for a good little grand piano, the casework was not relevant as it was to be painted white. A deal was struck with the Head Master. Me and Lesley loaded up the grand.

I called Joe the polisher in, and after a discussion he gave me a price to strip the casework, do any repairs and to spray the cabinet in white, hard wearing melamine paint. When the job was completed it looked a treat. A date was set to deliver the piano to the Midlands. Andy Taylor, the band's guitar player, was very pleased with his new piano. I became a little worried as when I was carrying the legs into his house I noticed, in the bright sunlight, a blush of pink. As soon as I got back to Devon, I went to see Joe the polisher, telling him about the change of colour. Joe said "It would probably be the red stain applied to the wood when the piano was new, and that red always bleeds". I fully expected a call saying the piano had turned pink. I was still making trips to the capital, tuning Ray Cooper's pianos, even fitting in jobs for Harvey Goldsmith. One day Ray Cooper called me asking me if I could drop everything and come to Henley on Thames where he was working with George Harrison in his studio. With the offer of a good cash return, I was on my way within the hour. It was a hot summer's day arriving at George Harrison's mansion. After pressing a button, a voice asked, "Can I help you?" I replied, "It's the piano tuner". The ornate, wrought iron gates opened. I drove in, following the pink gravel driveway, meandering through the stunning landscaped gardens. I parked up and knocked on the door. The door opened with a lady holding out her hand saying, "You must be Terry the Tuner". I was shown upstairs to where the piano was, a beautiful room with a stunning view overlooking the grounds. I had finished tuning the Steinway when George entered the room. He thanked me for driving all the way from Devon to tune his piano. I was paid by his secretary, in cash, as promised. I left the house and got in my car. As I drove away I looked in my mirror, and to my horror my car had left a black oil slick, the size of a large pizza on the pink gravel driveway. Whoooops!

I had settled into my new way of life. My journey to work was to just descend a flight of stairs into my workshop. I was enjoying working on all the different pianos made by English, German and French makers. Starting early in the morning, I would finish at lunchtime and spend the afternoons in the garden. I had planted an assortment of vegetables and now was making a wooden house for my newly acquired point of lay chickens to roost in. I had fenced off a good area at the end of the walled garden to stop the brood pecking at my vegetables. When I was doing any digging I would throw the odd worm into the chicken run causing a riot, feathers flapping in the chase to get to the worm first. I was collecting a half-dozen of the best eggs ever, everyday.

I had bought a pair of 1930's Bechstein baby grands. Both of these top quality instruments had ebonized cases. After Joe had repolished them back to a black lustre, and with the insides restored, I sold one of them to the Italian Ambassador. I delivered the instrument to London. My Bedford ambulance, which I had hand painted in dark blue, with the wheel arches covered in Devon mud looked utterly out of place outside the Italian Embassy. The other baby Bechstein was packed up in a wooden crate and sent to Washington DC, to a friend of Ray Cooper's.

After a couple of years Christine and I had grown apart and so we parted.

Living in the country doesn't suite everyone. I gave Christine a good sum of money to buy a house. By doing this, it put me in the red. I now had an overdraught with the bank.

As well as restoring pianos, I started the renovation of a newly acquired 1948 Rover. In the evenings I would spend my time recording music. Over the next three years I spent a lot of time improving my property and gardens. Finally, at the beginning of 1986, I decided to sell my house in order to pay back my ever increasing overdraft. I enjoyed my years living in the village of Chulmleigh, making many good chums.

BACK TO SOUTH DEVON

I moved to the town of Totnes hoping I would find more work in South Devon. I managed to buy an old detached house known as 'Gothic Lodge'. The whole of the property needed much work.

I rented a small workshop in the town centre and set about buying and selling pianos. Business was good and I would work on pianos in the daytime, working on my house in the evenings.

I had been approached by a man called Denis. He wanted a good quality grand piano for his recording studio. After discussing his budget, I told Denis that there were many excellent pianos other than the top known makes. After a couple of weeks, I had found an instrument, which I thought would make a good studio piano, a 1920's, 7ft Ronisch. After I had totally restored the German made grand, I called Denis. A deal was done.

Gothic Lodge, my house in Totnes

After Denis had written a cheque, he told me that there was no road access to 'Saw Mills Studios' and the only way to get the piano to the studio was by boat. I employed a local removal company. Denis had told me that we had to be at the quayside, on the River Fowey, in Cornwall, at the right time, so as to meet the high tide.

It was quite a job sliding the piano into the small open boat. All safely aboard, the grand piano, on its side, sticking up out of the boat like a shark's fin. We chugged up the river. After a mile or so, we had to go under a railway bridge. As we approached, it was obvious the piano was too high to go under the bridge. We bobbed about for over an hour, by which time the tide had dropped enough for us to pass under the bridge and into the wooded creek, the studio a short distance ahead. After the grand was safely installed, I set about tuning the piano ready for its first recording session. By the time I had finished it was low water and the only way out was by walking a mile down the railway line, back to my car. The little used branch line was only used by slow moving wagons filled with china clay.

After several days of torrential rain, I opened up my workshop one morning, to find the roof leaking water, causing severe damage to three out of four pianos I had in stock. The water damaged pianos had to be scrapped. Having no insurance, I was well out of pocket. I moved out of the workshop, putting all my time and effort into finishing my house. Yet again, I had to sell up and move so as to pay off my ever increasing debts.

The property in Totnes that I had renovated over the last five years had increased in value and after it had sold, there was sufficient money to buy a rural farmhouse in need of much work. The old house came with four acres of land plus an acre of woodland. After extensive work to my new house and converting an adjacent stable into a luxury extension, money was starting to run out.

1991 was my twenty-fifth year of working with pianos and I fancied a change. I had found for sale a 1946 Lea Francis estate car. The whole of the bodywork was made of wood. Over the years rot had set into most of the timbers, leaving just enough sound wood to make a template from. All new components I made out of seasoned ash, remaking the sixteen different walnut parts that made up the dashboard. It took almost a year to finish the restoration of the Lea Francis. I was asked by the 'National Motor Museum' if I would be interested in taking part in a cavalcade of rare classic cars. The journey from Devon to Bewley, in Hampshire, was made without a hitch. I received an accolade from the curator of the museum, for the quality of my work on the old shooting brake. All participants, taking part in the gathering of old unique cars received lunch with Lord Montague. Over the period spent working on the Lea Francis there had been several rises in interest rates and my overdraft with the bank, yet again, was getting out of control. It was time to start another piano shop.

Motorbiking, late 1980s

With the Lea Francis at Bewley National Motor Museum, 1991

The Lea Francis in Totnes

I found a suitable workshop in the old monumental stone-masons building, in the centre of Totnes, which had been converted into units. After meeting with Mike, the proprietor, I paid him a month's rent in advance. My new neighbours in the complex were a cabinet maker, dress maker, a man who repaired bicycles and upstairs was a hairdressers, run by a zany Scotsman, Joe.

I started to deal in more humble pianos as my accountant told me that, "This is the only profitable part of your business". The meticulous restoration of grand pianos was not profitable, spending months at a time with no income, then waiting for a customer to buy the finished instrument. I managed to buy an old Mercedes van. Being able to transport pianos myself made the difference between making a profit or paying a transport company and barely making wages.

The country was now in a recession. Interest rates had soared to an all-time high and the first thing to be hit were luxury goods, the sale of pianos withered. I tried to sell the Lea Francis without success. The bottom had dropped out of the classic car market.

Mike, the proprietor of the workshop complex, was in a dire financial state. He had the whole of the site of the stonemason's yard, on a long lease from the Co-op, who were the freeholders. Under the pressure, Mike became ill, suffering a heart attack. One morning he came and told everyone that he was throwing in the towel, as he was in arrears with the rent. While the other tenants went into panic mode, I telephoned the Co-op regional head office in Plymouth. I spoke to a man in the estate office. He was aware Mike had surrendered his lease. I asked if a new lease on the complex would be available and if so, how much? I received a letter from the Coop offering a new, twenty-one year lease.

I managed to pay all the legal cost and the first quarter's rent.

By now, my debts forced me to put my house up for sale. The worsening economic climate had severely hit the property market and house prices were starting to fall. Most of my tenants payed the rent, but there was always someone in financial difficulties. There was a detached outside building, in the yard, which was in need of renovation. I turned this space into a rehearsal room. There was a trickle of an income from local bands and musicians.

It was almost three years before I had an offer on my house, by which time all of my equity had been eroded. By the time the bank had been paid back, there was nothing left.

Having nowhere to live, I made a bedsit in the roof space, over the workshop.

Bill, an old friend from The Who days, was now working for the Rolling Stones. He had put my name forward to restore a baby grand for Keith Richards. The Challen baby grand Keith had bought new from Harrods in the 1960's. He had asked for it to be painted psychedelic. Harrods obliged his request and hired a student from one of the London art colleges, to undertake the task. I was told by Keith's office not to touch the casework and to only restore the inside workings of the piano. After the psychedelic grand arrived, I set straight to work. The renovation of the instrument was straightforward. There were many cigarette burns on the casework. After enquiring, I was told not to try and disguise the cigarette burns, but to leave them. I delivered the restored piano to Keith's house near Chichester. Sherry attended to Keith's affairs and she asked if I would look after the piano in the future. I told her just to call me when the piano needed tuning.

My Son Billy on top of the Keith Richards' psychedelic Challen

The income from the job soon got absorbed. I had lost half of my tenants, everyone hit by the deepening recession. The Co-op had informed me that if I was interested in buying the freehold of my Totnes premises, a figure of £50,000.00 would be acceptable. I went into overdrive, selling my collection of antique furniture. I also prepared my cherished Erard piano ready for sale. I had a meeting with a local architect. He looked around the dilapidated buildings making up the stonemasons yard. He told me with outline planning permission to redevelop the site; the value would be around £150,000.00. This was a chance to regain my fortunes. I applied for a commercial mortgage on the property.

The commercial funding company required a fee for arranging the loan. The amount they wanted was equal to a quarters rent. I decided to take a risk and use my rent money. I was offered a mortgage for £45,000.00. All I now needed was £5,000.00 to clinch the deal. I had paid back Lloyds bank the £130,000.00 I owed them, and felt sure they would lend me the £5,000.00 to secure the property. After application was made to the bank, I was refused the needed £5,000.00. I was gutted, I could not go forward with the purchase of the workshops, and to make things worse I couldn't pay the rent. I was also being hounded by the local council for £400.00 I owed in business rates. It was now the summer of 1996. I had been visited by the enforcement officer from the council. I explained to him that pianos did not sell during the holiday months of July and August and as soon as the children went back to school, there was always the sale of pianos to youngsters wanting to learn to play. My plea went on deaf ears. I was given ten days to pay the debt. I had two upright pianos possessed by the bailiffs. Each instrument I had bought and refurbished. The pair of uprights would have brought me in the best part of two thousand pounds. I received a letter from the enforcement officer, telling me that the pianos had been sold, at auction, for a hundred and ten pounds, the pair. I still owed the council two hundred and ninety pounds. After the refusal from the bank and the actions of the local authority, I had run out of options, the risk had not paid off. I had no option but to do a moonlight. I was lucky finding a building to rent on an isolated farm, some four miles out of the town. I did a runner from the stonemason's yard, moving my remaining belongings into the ancient barn. Having nowhere to live, I took up residence in the back of my old van.

My Erard 1910 Upright Piano

LIVING AS A HOBO PIANO TUNER

The first night I had to sleep in the back of my van was not very pleasant. Winter was coming on and the temperatures were dropping. Having little money, I managed to buy enough sheets of cheap plywood, to line the interior, top, bottom, and both sides of the back of my van. From the proceeds of a couple of piano tunings, I used contact adhesive to stick, dark red corduroy carpet to the whole of the interior. I used a whole sheet of plywood to make a raised bed, creating much needed storage space underneath. I designed the interior of my new home so everything could easily be removed, being able to move a piano. I was fortunate as the new 'Pay as You Go' mobile phones, were now available. I could now keep in contact with the outside world. One of the first calls I received on my new device was from Joe, the French polisher. He asked me if I would be interested in helping him to refinish the interior woodwork of an old house. I met Joe in the village of Silverton. I then followed him to the isolated Devon farmhouse. Joe introduced me to the owner, Mrs B. She was overseeing the restoration work being carried out. The farmhouse dated back to the fourteen hundreds. It had retained most of its original oak wall panelling, the low ceilings having massive oak beams supporting the floor above. Joe took me through the process of stripping and preparing the ancient timbers. I soon picked up the knack of refinishing the oak. Negotiating a good hourly rate with Mrs B, I arranged to spend a couple of days a week working on the oak.

I enjoyed my new routine of driving the fifty miles to Silverton. After a days work, the other tradesman working on the property went home at five o'clock leaving the whole place deserted. Half an hour later, I took the opportunity to use one of the finished bathrooms and have a good soak in hot water. Dressing in clean clothes, I walked the mile into the village, had an evening meal in one of the pubs and returned to my van for a good nights sleep.

After a few weeks, Joe did not want to carry on with the gruelling work and left me to finish the job. I took two months, sometimes spending the whole week working on the main sitting room of the house. The floor to ceiling panels, beams and oak floor glowed when I had finished. Mrs B lived in a Georgian mansion a few miles away. She knew my skills were in the piano trade and she asked if I could have a look at her Broadwood, square piano, dating back to 1820. I gave Mrs B a price to restore the early piano. I started working on the fragile period instrument.

On a visit to "Redlands", after tuning the psychedelic piano for Keith Richards, Sherry said, "Keith needed an upright piano for the cottage next door". I said, "I would try and find something interesting". Harris Osborn's, the music shop I had served my apprenticeship with, had closed down in the 1980's. The old craftsman, that I had been trained by were either, retired or dead, but there was a new piano shop in Paignton started up by Alan. Alan had been in the Royal Navy. After serving his term, he rented a small shop and filled it with second hand pianos. Alan, not being a piano man, employed local tuners to work on his stock. On a visit to Alan's shop, I was interested in a huge old American upright piano. After a haggle, a deal was done. I was to spend a day tuning Alan's stock in return for the American monster.

 I enjoyed working on the upright piano made in Chicago around 1905. I replaced all of the strings. The bass strings being equal, in length, to that of a six foot grand. I was confident enough to finish the casework myself, using plenty of red dye, mixed with the French polish. I took photographs of the finished piano, wrote a letter with details of the instrument and posted them off to Sherry. A week later I had a call from Sherry telling me that Keith would like to buy it. A few days later, I removed my bed and belongings, out of my van and with the help of my friend Dougie, we loaded the monster piano onto the back of my van and delivered it to Redlands. Keith was well happy with his new piano.

With some of the proceeds from the sale of the American upright, I bought a late 1950's classic caravan, with beautiful original wood interior and all mod-cons, including gas central heating. I had done extensive work on a baby grand piano for a client living in Dartmouth. He was finding difficulties in settling my bill. He asked me if I was interested in a boat. I was intrigued and made arrangements to view the craft. The only access to the boat was to walk through a half mile of woodlands, descending onto a small beach, in a deserted tidal creek off the river Dart. Ray and Janice had lived on the old boat for fifteen years bringing up their children in the isolated paradise. 'Leaway', was a 1959, twenty-seven foot cabin cruiser and in its day was a luxury mahogany boat, made by the top maker, 'Moody's'. I knew nothing about boats and after transferring the mooring, I took 'Leaway' as payment for the work carried out on Ray's baby grand. I lived in my caravan for the winter, spending all the summer months living on the boat. Three piano tunings per month covered all the money I needed to rent my workshop, cover the mooring of the boat and for a pitch on a rustic caravan site on the edge of Dartmoor, for my caravan.

Far from the madding crowd: Leaway my home on the Dart

My classic caravan on Dartmoor

I was now learning to slow down, spending days on end down the creek. I was living closer to nature, going to bed when the sun went down, rising at dawn, my south facing beach being bathed in sunshine the whole of the day. Included in the deal with Ray was an old fibreglass speedboat, originally having a huge seventy-five HP outboard engine, I only had a four HP Seagull engine, and a pair of paddles. On the high tide I would meander down the creek. I became skilled at knowing where the fish lurked, catching sea bass to order. In the main river I fished for mackerel. I had to return to my haven before the tide went out. At low water I collected cockles, mussels and oysters. Eating my fresh seafood creations, I started to realise I was living a better way of life. I would spend days on end living down the creek. The longest duration being eleven days, living in symbiosis with nature. When surfacing into the outside world, the first sensation driving into the town was the smell of exhaust fumes and how noisy the outside world was.

Whenever I had to go and tune a piano I would collect water from the fresh water stream, which came down through the woods. I would boil up the water and do my ablutions. Always keeping a change of clothes in my van, so I could look respectable in the outside world, which I now referred to as "The Madness!"

Me and Stuart with the Lea Francis

SERENDIPITY

Five years passed by living the feral life, I had developed a wild, weathered look, one immediately recognised people who also lived the outside life. I had survived three bouts of hypothermia. One cold, damp November I was visited by my friend Stewart, I was lucky as he found me fading in and out of consciousness. Stewart helped me walk up through the woods to his car, he then took me back to his flat in Totnes. It took me three days before I properly came round.

Then there was the time I developed a fungus growing in my skin. The condition was very painful, spreading all over my stomach, groin and down my legs. I visited my doctor, he was not sure what my condition was, conferring with a colleague, looking at pictures in reference books, trying to find which particular fungus had invaded my body. After three courses of antibiotics there was no improvement. The ailment was eventually cured using lavish amounts of tea tree oil. As I was starting to feel a little better, I started to lose my hair. It fell out in clumps, leaving me with just a whisper of remaining strands. I returned to the surgery where I saw a new doctor. I told her of my hair falling out and enquired could it be the antibiotics I had been taking. She checked out what pills I had been taking and she informed me that it was not known that any of the prescriptions I had taken had hair loss as a side effect. The doctor then said for my hair to fall out so quickly I had suffered more than stress, you must have suffered a trauma. I looked at the novice doctor and asked "Will it grow again?" With a forlorn look she replied "I don't know". I said to her "Don't worry there is magic mud down the creek. I will apply it to my head and my hair will grow again".

Walking through the market in Totnes, people stared at my emaciated appearance. I bumped into Margaret, one of my regular piano tuning clients. Margaret asked "What has happened to you?" She told me to eat lots of sunflower seeds. Over the next few weeks I applied the mud from the creek to my scalp, and also consumed large amounts of sunflower seeds. The potion worked, as a few weeks later my hair started sprouting and eventually grew back thicker and healthier than ever.

Leaway, my boat, was now starting to fall into disrepair. I had been tipped off that there was a boat for sale, moored in a small boatyard at the top of the creek. I went to investigate. John, the owner of the boatyard showed me "Merita", a gentleman's motor yacht. The forty-five foot vessel was built in Cornwall just after the war. Appearing to be in good condition with bronze port holes, shiny, mahogany woodwork and teak decks. John told me, the elderly owner had died and no one in the family wanted the boat. John then informed me that although the little ship appeared to be in good condition, the hull was fragile. The craft would be fine in the river but was not fit to go out to sea. "Marita" was tied up inside a dock and John said that it has to go because we need the space. John and I shook hands, a deal was struck. There was five hundred pounds owed to the boatyard. I managed to scrape together the five hundred pounds and I purchased my new vessel for the sum of one pound. I was informed by John that I had to remove "Marita" within three days. I started to move my belongings onboard as I prepared to leave the creek. I was joined by Stewart and a mutual friend Diana. She was a petite, well spoken lady several years my senior. Her passion was carving gem stones. She had recently returned

from Australia where she had been on an opal mining exped-
ition. Over the next couple of days Diana cooked delicious
vegetarian food, while Stewart and myself checked out the large
diesel engine, and also making sure the steering mechanism was
all in order. The day came for our departure. We could not leave
until high tide, which was at the latter end of the afternoon. I
was getting quite nervous, as I had never been behind the wheel
of such a large vessel. Not only that, she was tied up in an en-
closed dock. The bow of the boat, only inches away from the
dock wall, to starboard there was a walkway, the entire length
of the boat. At the stern of the boat, only inches away was a
floating dock. As high water approached I started the engine,
my nerves quite on edge. I was quite aware of the potential
damage I could do with a fifteen ton boat and the inertia behind
it. To make things worse there had gathered an audience of
boatyard workers. I was at the wheel; Diana had cast off the
rope in the stern, while Stewart pulled the bow of the boat, to
port, heaving the rope along the dock wall. As we cast off, Stewart jumped onboard. I pulled the gear handle into forward and
gently raised the 'revs'.

We slowly moved forward. I was now facing the side of a huge
passenger vessel, tied up in the adjacent boatyard. I put the
gear lever into reverse and raised the 'revs'. After several man-
oeuvres I safely negotiated the vessel out of the dock and into
the creek. There was a round of applause from our observers. I
felt a great sense of relief. I was familiar with the channel that
twisted and turned. Keeping to this contour, I steered the mile
or so down towards the main river into deeper safer water.

As we approached Sandquay, at the mouth of the creek, I looked
up at the Britannia Royal Naval College, where I used to tune
their pianos. It was one job I disliked. Gaining admittance,
going through security checks while the armed guards stared
with suspicion. There were old pianos, all of which were
clapped-out. The only decent instrument was in the Royal Mar-

ines Band room, a Yamaha grand. The Royal Marines Band, what a load of overweight loafers. Regarding being paid, they were one of the slowest. On writing on a duplicate invoice, I wrote, in fountain pen, "Could you please pay attention! To this unpaid bill!!!" I received a cheque by return-of-post; I never got any more jobs from the establishment. We steered to the left at the start of our journey up the river while I sat in the cockpit and smoked a cigarette. I was joined by Diana; we soaked up the stunning scenery. The sun was setting as we steamed into Totnes. I was back at the wheel, having to negotiate a mooring, against the outgoing tide. As soon as all the ropes were safely tied, we all took refreshment at the bar at the Royal Seven Stars Hotel in Totnes. The next day, Diana and Stewart had gone their ways. I was left alone rising and falling with the tide. I started to feel a little insecure, as I had no insurance and also the river dues had not been paid. I became more aware of the liability I had taken on. It was the end of the summer and the Autumnal chill settled early on the banks of the river. On the opposite bank, at the end of Canary Wharf, crowds of people waited to go through and view the new craft being built by the adventurer Pete Goss. I went to look at the enormous catamaran; it was an all new design and made of carbon fibre. Many stopped and admired my traditional boat, with its beautiful lines and gleaming woodwork.

As time passed by, I felt more insecure about the plight I had brought upon myself. After a sleepless night I had formulated a plan. I was going to try and sell "Marita" before the winter. The launching of Pete Goss's Team Philips high-tech Catamaran was about to happen. I cleaned and polished "Marita" and nailed a for sale sign to the mast. On the day of the launch there were crowds of people and television cameras. I sat and waited for any enquiries. Many people admired my classic boat. I saw people writing down my telephone number.

The day passed by and the catamaran was successfully

launched, starting its maiden voyage, slowly making its way down the river to Dartmouth, surrounded by a multitude of support vessels. The next day I received a phone call from a man called Dutch. He wanted to come the next morning and view "Marita". The next morning, I was sat drinking tea, when I could see a lone figure walking down the banks of the river. He came alongside and said, "Are you Terry?" as we shook hands Dutch came aboard. Dutch was of few words. The whole time he thoroughly inspected "Marita". After his inspection, Dutch joined me for a cup of tea, as he sat down, removing his cap, running his hand over his head, replacing his cap and now stroking his beard, he said "She needs some work, I'll offer you five thousand", "Go up five hundred and she's yours". Dutch held out his hand, we shook on the deal. He then pulled a wad of bank notes out of his pocket and counted out five hundred pounds, handing me the money he said "I'll be back the day after tomorrow". When Dutch was out of sight, I jumped for joy with excitement. What a profit. I had money in my pocket and in a couple of days nowhere to live. Later the same day, I was tuning a piano in Alan's Piano shop in Paignton. I told Alan of the sale of my boat. Alan then said that he had a flat to let. The same evening, I went to view the flat at Alan's house. Alan's house was a crumbling, detached Victorian mansion which stood on a hillside, in the middle of half an acre of walled garden, with uninterrupted sea views.

Alan showed me the basement. There was a good sized kitchen, a bedroom with en suite shower and toilet. The sitting room was good sized, with a baronial sized fireplace. Alan told me the rent was sixty pounds a week, with pound coins in the metre for electricity. The simplicity of Alan's terms suited me very much. I arranged to move in. My last night on board "Marita" was very cold. The next day Dutch turned up and counted out five thousand pounds in cash. I recounted the notes and wrote out a receipt for the money and gave it to Dutch. I had previously removed all my belongings and put them in my car. We shook hands and I left Dutch on board "Marita".

Manoeuvring Marita up the river Dart

BACK TO DRY LAND

Arriving at my new abode I opened the kitchen door. This was a strange feeling, even just having a front door key. I immediately opened all of the windows. On entering the sitting room, there was my old Chesterfield. Alan had bought my beloved Chesterfield when I left my farmhouse. I had originally acquired the Chesterfield from Shepperton Studios, it had been a prop in many films, when I rescued it from the roadies restroom, on stage 'M', The Who's studio. Battered and threadbare, I knew it was a classic. When I first left London I had the whole thing re-sprung and re-upholstered at great cost. It was very strange to be surrounded by walls after my time outdoors. I now had the luxury of hot and cold running water and electric lights instead of oil lamps. I kept the windows permanently open, taking nothing for granted, I did not want to get too comfortable in case I had to return to the outdoors. I was now working a couple of days a week in Alan's piano shop. A morning's work covered my rent on my flat; the remainder covered my weekly needs.

In the New Year, I decided to put my stash of money to work. Firstly, buying an old Mercedes minibus, from an old people's home in Somerset. I removed all of the rear seats; this vehicle was now a piano removal van as well as a mobile home.

There was no shortage of wood to burn on my open fire, as the market for pianos was forever diminishing. Alan and myself started chopping up old and past it grand's and uprights. As I burned old sets of piano keys and casework timbers, I gazed into the flames thinking of the old piano men that made these old instruments, and of the homes these piano's had been cherished in.

One day on my return home there was a very large upright piano in the middle of the driveway. I raised the lid and on the fall was the maker's name, inlaid, Gothic styled brass letters Ritmmuler, a make of piano that I was not familiar with. I peered into the inside, the hammers had had very little use, although quite dusty. The instrument was way out of tune. Even so the tone of the monster was remarkable. I asked Alan what he was going to do with the Ritmmuler. He replied "Yours for a hundred quid". Half an hour later the piano was in my sitting room. I set about reviving the instrument. I stripped down the action, removing all the hammers and dampers. Although there was little wear on the felts and leathers, the damper springs, spiral springs and repetition springs needed replacing. Within a week I had re-assembled the action, cleaned out the inside of the instrument, polished the ivory keys and attended to the regulation. Now it was time to tune the Ritmmuler. I raised the pitch to A 440. By the time I had finished the second tuning I realised I had a very special piano. This 1920's, German made piano was one of the best instruments that I had ever worked on and what a delight to play.

As the digital age was taking over the world, I managed to buy the new ways of recording music. A multi-track digital recording station along with one of the few things that I had ever bought new, a Yamaha digital keyboard, with sampled piano sounds plus strings, brass instruments, saxophones and a range of synthesized sounds. I now spent my evenings making music, being able to lay down track after track, compiling pieces of music. I would spend hours improvising, trying new ideas.

Years previous, one would need thousands of pounds for equipment to do this. Now it cost just hundreds.

Before the money ran out from the sale of "Marita", I managed to find my next project, a 1960's, model K, upright Steinway. The owners had the instrument from new. On inspection of the workings of this fine piano, I could see the sound board and bridges were in excellent condition, as was the condition of the action. Unfortunately the ivory keys were in poor condition, as was the casework, although there was no damage, the original finish was very tired. I made an offer of twelve hundred pounds. The owner said he would let me know. A couple of days later I had a call from the owner of the model K Steinway, saying he had another offer of fifteen hundred pounds. I replied that I would raise my offer to one thousand, six hundred and fifty pounds. An hour later I received a phone call saying that my offer would be acceptable.

The piano was collected and delivered to my workshop. I dismantled the casework, removed the action and keys. With all the tricks of the trade I gave the strings, wrest pins, iron frame, soundboard and bridges a thorough clean and polish. After just one day's work the whole inside of the instrument looked like the day it was made. I removed any salvageable ivory key tops, parcelled up all of the natural keys and sent them for re-covering; the specialist firm replaced all the natural keys with grained celluloid, a synthetic substitute for ivory.

The action of the piano I stripped down. The hammers had plenty of felt, having had little wear. After careful re-facing, they looked as new. Within a week all the workings of the instrument were finished. All I needed to complete the job was the return of the keys. As funds were now exhausted I could not pay for Joe the polisher to re-finish the casework. There was no alternative, I had to tackle the job myself. I started to strip the casework. First I coated one panel at a time with stripper, leaving it to bite in for a good fifteen minutes. I then re-coated the first panel with a second coat of stripper. Then I carefully pushed a scraper over the wood, removing the old cellulose finish, a scrub down with coarse wire wool and to my delight the process had revealed the beautiful, fiddle-back mahogany.

After a good days work, all of the casework was ready for the process of re-finishing. I laboured for over a month, coat after coat of the finest French polish was applied. The keys had now returned, so while giving the finished casework time to go really hard, I set about regulating the action and keys, followed by tuning the instrument to concert pitch. I then spent two days, carefully voicing the hammers.

It was now time to finish the casework. First of all I polished all of the brass work, pedals, hinges, locks and every brass screw head. All of the panels and parts had to be burnished to a high lustre. When the model K was finished, it looked and sounded stunning. Now it was time to make a sale. Placing an advert in the Western Morning News, with the price of eight thousand, five hundred pounds. There were many phone calls. I was not surprised. Most enquiries amounted to just a long chat about pianos. Even though the price was way on the low side, it was too much for a piano advertised in the classifieds of a provincial newspaper. A month passed and I had still not managed to find a customer. I was now on the bottom of my pocket. I decided to call Steinways in London. I spoke to the manager, an American man called Ron Losby, telling him of the upright model K and also that I had served with the company almost forty years ago. He asked me if there were any splits in the sound board and were the bridges in sound condition. I assured him that all was in first-class order. Finally, he asked if I could e-mail him some pictures of the instrument. Not having a computer or digital camera, Alan obliged by taking pictures and e-mailing them to Ron Losby. The very next day I received a call from the manager of Steinways. He told me he liked the look of the piano and if it was as good as it looked he could offer me six thousand pounds for the instrument. I had no other option so I accepted the offer.

Two days later I was on my way to London, driving my old Mercedes, with the Steinway secured in the back. I was accompanied by my friend Chris, a young man who was learning the piano trade, working in Alan's piano shop. We found our way to Steinway Hall, which was now situated in Marylebone Lane, having moved from Mayfair to the new premises just north of Oxford Street some years previous. These new premises much glossier than the sober Steinway Hall I had served at.

I entered the glossy building and asked to see Mr Losby. While waiting I wandered around looking at the new instruments. I was then approached by an immaculately dressed man, holding his hand out, he said "Ron Losby". I told him the piano was in my van outside. "Let's have a look" he said. Chris had removed all the ties and blankets. With just a glance Mr Losby said "Ah, yes, wheel it in through the front door". Chris and myself heaved the heavy instrument out of the van and through the doors into the foyer of Steinway Hall. Ron greeted us holding the front door open, saying "Put it over there", the Steinway piano I had restored was to be placed in the most focal point as people entered Steinway Hall. I removed the front panel for my work to be inspected by the manager of Steinways, together with an in-house technician, who I recognised from all those years before when I served with the company. After the two had finished their inspection, Ron Losby shook my hand saying "You're a man of your word, no splits in the sound board and a first-class job. Come to my office I will write you a cheque". Sharing a pot of tea with Ron, he asked me about the time I was working for the company. I reflected on the lessons I was given in tuning from Bob Glazebrook and of being present when John Lennon came in to buy his piano and of Mr Allan's disapproving tone when he said he wanted it in white. When returning downstairs the model K seemed to have a glow from the hand finished lustre, rather than just a shine of the polyester finished new pianos.

On my return to Devon, I deposited the cheque from Steinways into my bank account. It was now just a few days to wait to be lifted out of penury. Less than a week later, I received a call from the technician that I had recognised at Steinways. He told me the model K had been sold. The buyers of the instrument were from Highgate, but the upright piano was not for their North London home, it was to be installed in their house in Salcombe, South Devon. I chuckled at the irony. I then asked him how much it sold for. With some hesitation and dulcet tone, he said "A little over eighteen thousand pounds".

FORTY YEARS

I t's the beginning of December 2005, traditionally the busiest time of year for the piano trade. The piano I am tuning is a straight strung, over damper, a cheaply made instrument manufactured by the thousands some eighty years ago in various London factories.

The humble piano, like many other survivors, with little maintenance and a good tuning is still giving a lot of pleasure to its present owners. A bunch of musicians and song writers sharing a large rambling flat known as boogie H.Q. Totnes. As I ascended the tuning of the treble end of the piano the aroma of coffee percolating wafted round the L-shaped sitting room where a multitude of musical instruments laid in wait to be played. Looking dazed from the previous night's jam session one of the occupants handed me a coffee saying, "Morning man", at this moment my phone started to ring. On answering, a husky voice said "Hello Terry it's Heather, Sherry's assistant from Monro Sound. Could you please tune the pianos at Redlands on Thursday?" she asked. "Of course", I reply, "Will Sherry be there". Heather said that Sherry would be there at 11.30 am and that Mr and Mrs Richards would be in residence. I told Heather that I would be there for 10.00 am on Thursday.

I was fortunate that I was able to borrow a car for the day, for the trip to Redlands, as my only other mode of transport was my old piano delivery van, as well as being a gas guzzler, hand painted and rusty, it looked more befitting to have been parked on a traveller's site. I started my journey from Devon to Sussex well before dawn. As I travelled east parallel to the Jurassic coast of Dorset, the Sun made its lazy winter appearance on the horizon. I was thinking of Heather's remark, "Mr and Mrs Richards would be in residence". In all the years I had been tuning the pianos at Redlands I had never heard such a reference. On my arrival the gates of the large thatched house were open. I parked the car, then, tool case in hand, I walked through the fortress style wooden gates, over the ornamental moat and into the garden. The gardener, whom I had met on many previous visits, was trimming various bushes and shrubs with a pair of old fashioned shears. I wished him good morning and asked who was in. He replied "Bill and Doris". I knocked on the oak door at the rear of the house and as the door opened, I was greeted by an elderly man. "My name is Terry and I've come to tune the pianos", he replied "Ah yes, Terry, we're expecting you. My name is Bill, please come in". As I entered through the kitchen door Bill introduced me to the family gathering. Then from a wing-backed chair in the adjacent sitting room came a voice "Hello Terry, I'm Doris, Keith's mum". Bill escorted me through the house to the room where the psychedelic baby grand piano stood. A short while after starting to tune the piano, Bill returned with a mug of tea. We chatted for a while and in the conversation he told me it was forty years ago that Keith had bought the house. The thought passed through my mind, it was forty years ago that I had started in the piano trade. Sherry then arrived accompanied by her husband and their dog, Skippy. After her greeting I carried on tuning. As I was finishing the last notes in the bass section I heard someone behind me. I turned round to be greeted by Doris approaching with her arms in the air doing a shuffle dance singing "I can't get no satisfaction". Doris told me she was 91. I was amazed and said so. Doris then told me that she had good genes from some member of the family and six sisters. I muttered "Your poor Dad". Sherry then gathered everyone for a lunch outing. She paid me my money and joked about failing again to produce a receipt. I was then given two bunches of keys, one set to lock-up the house and the other keys to open the cottage nearby where I was to tune the second piano. As the cars pulled away I was left with only Skippy, Sherry's dog. After replacing various photographs on the baby grand, I locked up the house accompanied by Skippy.

I walked the short distance to the cottage, unlocked the door and entered. I pulled off the dust sheet to reveal the enormous American upright piano, which I was also familiar with because I had sold it to Keith. He had never come to look at the piano and purchased it from a few photographs and a letter. The monster upright was made in Boston USA. I had totally restored the instrument and the replacement bass strings were as long as those on a six-foot grand piano. On my return to the main house, I put the kettle on and made a cup of tea. A while later, Skippy started barking. He had heard a car approach. Bill and Doris returned from their lunch and Skippy was rewarded with a doggy bag. I finished my tea, said goodbye to everyone and started my journey back to Devon. As the miles ticked by, I thought back to Bill informing me Keith had bought the house forty years ago. It was at the same time, in 1966, that I had started my apprenticeship in the piano trade, forty years ago. I then thought of what a pleasure it was to meet Keith Richard's mum.

As the New Year started, it became evident the piano trade was in serious decline. Alan, being the canny Devonshire man, decided to put his piano shop and piano business up for sale. Within a few months the business changed hands. The new owner was a saxophone player, with dreams of being a piano shop proprietor. He failed miserably and the business closed within a few months.

With my income now much diminished I decided it was time again to find somewhere cheaper to live. Over the years, since I had lost my house and business, I had worked harder than I had ever worked, trying to re-establish myself. Every time I had made a little money there was a period of no work, using my savings to live on. I decided to go and have a look down the creek, to see if there were any suitable boats for sale. I was lucky finding "Sarah Louise", a twenty-eight foot, gaff-rigged sailing boat, with a sound hull, but needing some deck repairs. I paid just three hundred pounds for my new home. This time the boat came with a pontoon mooring, having electricity and water, and the rent was only fifteen pounds a week. Within a week I had moved aboard. As I left Alan's flat I closed all of the windows.

As the years passed by I withdrew more and more from the outside world. I spent my time rebuilding "Sarah Louise", using the hard woods I had collected over the years. I hated to see good wood go to waste. I was driving through the town of Totnes when I passed a skip outside Lloyds bank. The whole of the original mahogany interior had been ripped out of the bank. Later, the same day, I returned, rescuing the precious wood. Now most of that wood was given a second life in my boat.

REFLECTIONS

Over the next decade most provincial piano shops had gone out of business. The last British piano manufacturing company, Kemble, closed its doors in 2009. I managed to make a living having a good number of regular piano tunings.

There was now a lot of competition from the new age of piano tuners, having done a college course, leaving after a couple of years. Many of these new tuners boasted their qualifications, letters after their name and all of them attaining a diploma of merit. These feebly trained, so-called tuners helped the demise of the piano, leaving instruments sounding short of their potential beauty.

The year 2010, I returned to Dartington Hall, preparing pianos for the International Summer School, working on the same instruments that I had worked on over forty years before, amongst them there was an old Steinway model C grand which I fully restored.

For the six-week duration of the summer schools, there were up to forty pianos to keep in tune. I worked alongside Rodney. Rodney had served his apprenticeship with Blüthners. After finishing his apprenticeship in the 1970's, Rodney spent many years travelling around America tuning pianos. He now lived in London, looking after the pianos at Trinity College. It was a pleasure meeting Rodney, he was the only contact with the old school of piano men I had had in years.

I am now in my fiftieth year making a living, working with pianos. I have been able to tell my story of the years in London, as all my diaries, alongside with many letters and stage passes still survive. The rest is purely from memory. I have counted from my diaries the documented studio pianos I tuned, throughout the nineteen seventies, totalled two thousand six hundred and fifty-one recording sessions. Over one thousand one hundred live concerts. There were many more not written down, nice little cash jobs. I have very little to show for fifty years work, Albert was right, or was he! Learning my skill gave me my independence over the years, through the ups and downs.

My life would have been entirely different if my Mother had not seen the 'Ad', "Young man wanted to learn to become a piano tuner".

On the first Monday after my 65th Birthday, I had completed fifty years in the piano industry. Tuning pianos, repairing pianos, regulating pianos, restringing and restoring pianos, buying and selling pianos and the best part, playing pianos. Unlike Mr John Allen, the salesman at Steinways, he had a small red enamelled badge, presented to him by Mr Henry Steinway for fifty years' service. I recall thinking at the time, a little red badge for fifty years. On my fiftieth anniversary of serving in the piano trade I received nothing! Not a pat on the back, not a hand shake, not a phone call, congratulating me on my half century of service to music. During this fifty-year period, I had tuned pianos for some of the world's most famous Artists, entered the homes of the wealthiest people, pianos I had tuned still ring out on many of the world's most famous recordings. I may add, I gave my full attention to all pianos, not only the high end but giving my best to the humblest upright.

When I first set out tuning pianos, after serving my apprenticeship, the older generation had a good idea of whether a piano was in tune or not, for most of them could play. When I was an apprentice piano man, a high-quality piano was not out of the realms of attainability for an aspiring musician. Now such an instrument can only be acquired by the people who have pots of money. Very few of these people can play the piano, let alone know whether a piano was in tune. Many a fine instrument lies dormant in the homes of people with money and barely ever played, this to me is a madness. The only positive thing is that the skill of the men and women who make these fine instruments is still being passed on. The skills of great instrument makers can only be passed on in a working environment and not a in a place of education. Such a fine instrument I had stored in my father's garage. This piano was known as the Barless Broadwood, a grand piano where there are no cross members in the iron frame, this gave the instrument a continuity of tone, not like most other pianos where there are cross members strengthening the iron frame. The notes adjacent to the cross members can have a strange tone and reducing the length of the decay after a note is struck, also some of the notes can sound false, this was not a problem with the Barless Broadwood.

I was intending to restore this fine instrument, but it was not to be. The period was the end of the century. My mother had dementia and had moved into a nursing home. I was living on a boat and at this time had no workshop, so when this fine piano came my way, the only place to put it was in the dry garage at my parent's house. One day I received a manic message from my father that he wanted the grand piano out of his garage. I found out later he wanted the space so his new-found friend could keep her car in the dry. This new-found friend was a woman many years younger than he or me. She helped my father in the garden. He wanted to impress her, before I could find anywhere to put my Barless Broadwood my dad took a sledgehammer to this fine instrument, smashing it to pieces and taking bit by bit to the local refuge dump. Lightening had struck twice in the same place as it resurrected the memory of him smashing my guitar over my head many years before. He was in his late seventies when he destroyed any respect that I had left for him.

Another madness regarding the piano maker Broadwood was that in the years of the First World War, Broadwoods stopped making pianos giving the skilled workforce the task of making by-planes, actually making aeroplanes out of wood and canvas, so they could drop bombs on the enemy. The enemy being skilled craftsmen, German piano makers, instrument and furniture makers. What madness to make craftsmen and artisans of different nationalities kill each other. Many of the instruments made by German, English and French craftsmen of this period still survive and give pleasure to people to this day. Whenever I tune one of these instruments, I sometimes think of the men who made them and of the memory of Harry, the elderly piano tuner who survived the trenches of World War One and helped me as a young man learn my trade.

Of the many characters that I have met or worked for throughout my fifty years in the piano trade, Reva Gordon, the piano teacher come piano dealer was one of the shiniest, she knew how to greet people. She was unaffected by wealth or status. I always enjoyed seeing here either it be tuning pianos or just popping round to see her. Reva had gone from strength to strength dealing pianos from her apartment in Maida Vale, to acquiring an old piano factory in Camden Town. The large Victorian building just off Bayham Street, where many piano makers had come and gone. On occasion I would pay her a visit. She now had a stock of over one hundred upright and grand pianos, with a staff of French polishers, stringers and one of Reva's best technicians was a very attractive woman from Poland. I had never met a lady piano technician before, her work was as good as it can get. Reva's business was very healthy and over the years she must have sold hundreds of pianos.

It was years later I heard that Reva had got into a terrible mess with her finances and she was being hounded by the Inland Revenue. Not being able to handle the pressure and being the stylist that she was, checking into the Savoy Hotel, taking a suite, ordering the best on the menu on room service and then with copious amounts of champagne Reva washed down a bottle of pills. She even committed suicide in great style. To me this was a great tragedy. Reva Gordon was one of life's joyous people, for all the pianos that she had bought and sold, she had not made a great fortune, living in the same rented apartment and driving the same modest car.

The most musical creatures in our world are the birds, they sing for the sheer joy of being able to do so. Unfortunately, the number of birds, even in my lifetime, have plummeted. When I was young a short journey in the average car, throughout the summer months, one would have to scrape the windscreen of airborne creatures which had been splattered to death obscuring one's vision. These insects were the plankton of the air feeding abundant numbers of birds. Most of these insects have virtually disappeared, along with the birds and bats which fed upon them. Modern farming techniques are responsible for the tragedy.

I would like now to recall when I lost two pianos and a brand-new washing machine to the bailiffs, as I could not pay a four hundred- and ten-pounds business rates bill. I had explained to the enforcement officer, when the two pianos were sold, I could pay the bill in full, the two pianos were worth around eighteen hundred pounds to me. The enforcement officer gave me too little time and had the pianos re-possessed. The two pianos and a washing machine were sold at an auction for a total of one hundred and ten pounds leaving me still with a debt to the council of three hundred pounds. A few years later there were complaints of noise in town. The noise was a dozen or so Peacocks, which came over the wall from the Zoo in Paignton. These beautiful birds would be seen around the area, and it was a treat to see the male birds display their full majesty of feathers. Whenever it was the Peacocks mating season their call could be heard in the area of Paignton Zoo. The enforcement officer, who gave me little time to sell my pianos, lived on a housing estate close to the perimeter of the Zoo. He made a complaint to the council about the calls of the Peacocks. That mean-spirited man was responsible for the culling of a dozen Peacocks. What hope, what madness!

Over the years, the number people that could really play the piano diminished. One such piano player, in the seaside town of Paignton was Pam the pianist. Pam always greeted people with the same beaming smile, for a woman, at a guess, in her seventies. She dressed in a style of the nineteen fifties and always with her blonde hair in a ponytail of the era. Pam played in the pubs and hotels around Torbay. She had to play some pretty shabby pianos, I know because I had to tune them. Pam had a natural talent, playing without the printed music, all the songs from the great musicals to pieces of classical music, Debussy, Mozart and Gershwin. She also kept up with the latest pop songs and wherever she played there was always a singsong.

Another great pianist I tuned for was Chris Johns, he taught piano at his house in Totnes. His piano was a nineteen sixties Bechstein upright, also he had a studio in Plymouth where he kept his Bosendorfer grand. Over the years I tuned pianos for Chris, he became aware of the diminishing quality of piano tuning and maintenance. Chris was involved with Plymouth University. When I went to tune either of his pianos, he would tell me of how bad the pianos were in the music department of the faculty. After, at least, a couple of years he managed to get the university to get me to look at the instruments. An appointment was made. I was to meet the technician who looked after the musical instruments. I was on time, nine a.m., he was late. He was not very friendly. He told me that all the pianos were only seven years old and were regularly tuned.

He showed me into the universities recording studio where there was a six foot Yamaha grand. I played a chord, "Oh dear" I said, the technician asked me what was wrong. I told him the piano sounds awful. I told him the piano was severely out of tune, the regulation needed attending to and the hammers were in dire need of being toned. The technician then asked me, in a sarcastic tone, "What would be involved in doing the job?". I told him I could do the work today and also told him how much. He then said, "You better get on with it", he then walked out the door.

I set to work, first of all I tuned the Yamaha grand. By the time I had set the piano in tune, the morning had passed by. I then set about regulating the action, raising the blow, this simple adjust-ment, turning the capstone screws, bringing the hammers back into position, so as all the other functions of the action fall back into place. There was one more mechanical adjustment which was the damper stop bar. This particular adjustment is one of the simplest on a grand piano and can make such a difference to the touch. After this simple adjustment it was time for lunch. On my return I spent the rest of the day voicing the instrument. The piano had been played for hours every day. Slowly the hammers had become so hard the piano sounded nasty. Around four-thirty pm I was satisfied with the sound and the feel of the instrument. I went to find the musical technician, on our return to the recording studio, I asked him to try the piano, and he asked me if I could demonstrate it to him. I sat on the piano stool and purposely looked at the man's face as I struck the first notes, his draw dropped and his eyes widened, I carried on playing. I played hard and then dropped the tone to pianis-simo. When I finished playing, the musical technician's attitude completely changed. His first remark was he did not know that could be done to a piano, changing the sound from nasty to beautiful. Then he said how soon could you attend to the rest of the pianos. There was another Yamaha grand and several Ya-maha uprights all needing the same treatment.

This was not an isolated case, I was called by a music teacher from one of South Devon's Grammar Schools, all of the instruments there were in such a bad condition I felt sorry for the pupils trying to learn.

One could never make a fortune tuning pianos. The piano trade always fell far behind when compared with other trades. Piano tuners, instead of uniting together and all charging roughly the same price, would compete, bringing the charge for a tuning down. This, in my opinion, also lead to the diminishing standards of work. The unbeknown public would pick the cheapest price, and most of the time would have a piano still out of tune after the piano tuner had left. On answering the telephone to a new customer, many would ask "How much?". I would tell them my fee. On occasion the reply was "What! Just to tune a piano". When I heard this, I used to just hang up.

When I was a young man working in London, I would regularly be given a tip. The best tip I ever received was for a tuning at the Royal Albert Hall. It was the mid-nineteen seventies. The charge for a tuning was between four and five pounds. I was charging four pounds fifty. I had arrived a little early at the Royal Albert Hall. The band was in full swing and the singer was Frank Sinatra, the musicians, many of them from the USA. What a slick sound! The sound check over I went straight out on the concert platform and headed towards the piano, the atmosphere was electric. I caught a glimpse of Frank Sinatra in his double-breasted suit and black patent shoes, he was having the crack with his musical director. As I was tuning the higher treble of the piano, Mr Sinatra started to walk in my direction. I stopped tuning and stood up. We shook hands and he put something in my breast pocket and said, "Thanks Sonny" and immediately turning around, left the stage with his entourage. I carried on tuning. Only when I had finished did I look to see what he had put in my pocket. To my surprise it was a fifty-dollar bill, I could not believe it. A tip for over ten times my tuning fee.

One of the reasons that I decided to leave London in the early nineteen eighties, was that of traffic. I seemed to often be caught up in some traffic jam, fretting about getting to the next piano tuning. One thing I really hated was being late, whether the job was a concert, recording session or a piano in a private house. Over the years, the madness, that I tried to escape, has consumed every corner of the country.

Over the years I have been asked many times "Which make of piano was the best?". To say any one make of piano was the best I would consider to be quite ridiculous! Give me any make of piano well prepared, over a top mark piano which has been poorly maintained. Also, certain moods of music sound much nicer on a more desirable instrument.

Harmony, I have spent the whole of my working life trying to create harmony, whilst being surrounded in a world full of discord. The majority of discord is created by Humanity. Throughout my half-century of attending to pianos, I have been fortunate in meeting people of interest. Of the places I have tuned pianos, some of the wealthiest people I have met have been the most humble, while some of the people who work for the rich can be the most loathsome of beings. Throughout my fifty-year career I have experienced riches to rags. The years of making lots of money, I look back at this period as having been blinkered by money. Although life was hard, living a semi-feral existence, this experience taught me to respect the natural world. When I was very young in the nineteen fifties, my Mother pointed out to me the belching fumes pumped out by industry and vehicles. During the early nineteen seventies we were told of acid rain, killing trees and affecting our oceans. Instead of taking notice, the people in charge, all over the world, promoted bigger motorcars and more aeroplanes. It has taken millions of years to create the paradise that has evolved over the little blue planet in the universe and in no time at all, man and his Gods, Guns and Greed have ruined it. I look down at the loud and greedy and the show-offs. There is no harmonious future while these values rule... THE MADNESS.